Walking in the Truth

Walking in the Truth

A Companion Study
to *Lies Women Believe*

Nancy Leigh DeMoss

MOODY PUBLISHERS

CHICAGO

© 2002 Nancy Leigh DeMoss

Published by Moody Publishers.

Produced with the assistance of The Livingstone Corporation. Project staff includes Paige Drygas, Katie Gieser, Ashley Taylor, Linda Taylor, and Andrea Reider. Interior Design by Liita Forsyth.

Library of Congress Cataloging-in-Publication Data

ISBN: 0-8024-4692-2

7 9 10 8

Printed in the United States of America

Contents

Acknowledgments

I love being a part of the body of Christ. Thanks to the godly, gifted men and women He has placed around me, I have never had to give a "solo performance." As with every aspect of my life and ministry, this book has been a team effort. I am particularly grateful for . . .

- My dear friends and fellow servants at Moody Press. Heartfelt thanks to Greg Thornton, Bill Thrasher, Elsa Mazon, and Dave DeWit for the time and attention you have given to this project and for the personal and practical support you have provided at so many crucial points in the process.

- The Livingstone Corporation. Thanks especially to Linda Taylor for your help in developing the format and content for this study. And thanks to Paige Drygas for your editorial efforts and administrative assistance that have kept us all on track.

- My family, friends, and staff. Thanks for praying, encouraging, covering the bases in my extended absences from the office, dropping off meals, and even decorating my house for Christmas!

Thank you all for believing in this message and for the sacrifices you have made so it could be communicated to others. The women's lives that will be set free through this study are the fruit of your combined labors and loving investment.

Introduction

Since the original release of *Lies Women Believe,* we have received many encouraging responses from women describing the impact this message is having on their thinking and their walk with God. Women of every age, in every season of life, are having their eyes opened to the lies they have believed and are being set free by the Truth. One woman, a longtime friend, wrote the following:

> I cannot tell you the depth of work God is doing. Frankly, I am appalled at what lies I have allowed to permeate my thinking and subsequently have become my lifestyle. The thing that is so thrilling is to finally be able to identify those lies and to discover what hope there is in the Truth of God's Word to deliver me from the lies.

Many women are finally "connecting the dots"—realizing how deception in one area has consequences in other areas of their lives, as illustrated by this testimony:

> As I approach sixty years of age, I have seen that episodes of "depression" and longstanding struggles with anxiety are rooted in my misunderstandings about the character and nature of God.

Some have shared honestly that it was not an easy book to read. One woman phrased it this way: "It was like having a 'spiritual root canal'—only on my *heart.*" Now that's not the kind of testimonial that generally motivates people to read a book! However, she went on to express the blessing she is experiencing as a result of walking through the pain:

> I am learning to cherish the Word. There is such great joy in drinking deeply of it; it satisfies my longings, cleanses my mind, and leaves me craving more!

I have been especially glad to learn of women who are meeting together in small group settings to read and discuss the book. Again, the reports have been so encouraging. One woman told us that in her group "women are opening up and revealing lies they didn't even realize were lies and are able to face the lies with God's Truth."

We have received many calls and inquiries asking about the availability of a study guide to help women who want to go deeper in understanding and applying the message of *Lies Women Believe*. *Walking in the Truth* is designed for this purpose. It can be used for individual study or by a group of women who want to go through *Lies Women Believe* together.

If possible, I would encourage you to do this study with others—whether a Sunday school class, a Bible study group, or one or two other women who want to grow in their walk with God. A group setting will provide encouragement as you grapple with some of the lies that may be deeply imbedded in your thinking and will offer personal accountability as you seek to root out those lies and begin to walk in the Truth.

Whether you use this resource alone or with others, and whether you do it in ten weeks as suggested or at a slower pace, my prayer is that you will make the effort to take this journey out of deception and into the Truth. As you read and reflect and respond, open your heart to the Lord; ask Him to open your eyes—to show you where you may have been subtly deceived. Then trust Him to show you how to walk in the Truth and how to point others to the Truth that can set them free.

No matter how challenging or difficult the walk may prove to be at points, He has promised to walk with you. He will be your constant Companion, Guide, Helper, and Friend all the way till the end of the journey and then through all eternity!

How to Get the Most out of This Study

Walking in the Truth is designed to be a companion study to the book *Lies Women Believe*. You will need to have a copy of the book in order to follow along in the study. You do not need to read the entire book before beginning this study; instead, you will be assigned a few pages in the book to read along with each day's study. In this way, you will read the entire book, but in small portions at a time as they apply to the day's study.

Each chapter includes the following features:

- **In a Nutshell**—An introductory section that gives you an overview of the chapter and the lies discussed in that chapter.

- **Exploring the Truth**—Five days of personal study for you to complete during the course of the week between your small group meetings. Completing these lessons will give you time to personally think through how to incorporate God's truths into your daily life. Each day's study includes a few pages to read from *Lies Women Believe* and then questions to answer under the subtitles "Realize," "Reflect," and "Respond." You will need your Bible, because each lesson includes verses to look up.

- **Walking Together in the Truth**—Questions to be discussed when your small group meets. If you are not doing this as part of a group study, then simply use this section as an extra day or two of personal study. The questions are different from what is in the other lessons and will continue to challenge you to think deeply and to consider personal application.

Take your time as you do these studies. The questions are meant to challenge you and force you to think through your attitudes and beliefs. Some of these questions may be difficult for you. To be honest, I hope they are. Without pain, we can't experience change; and without change, we cannot hope to grow. As you sense God working in your heart, you will want to spend time in prayer to consider what God wants to teach you.

If you miss a day, don't give up! Bible study is a discipline, but it yields abundant fruit for those who are willing to pay the price. Try to set aside some quiet moments each day to read, reflect, and respond to the questions in this guide. May the Lord bless your desire to follow Him and walk in the freedom of His Truth.

Laying the Foundation

In a Nutshell . . .

The Introduction and chapter 1 lay a foundation for understanding the power of Satan's lies in our culture and in our personal lives and for discovering the far more powerful Truth as found in God's Word. A fatal flaw that is embraced by our culture is to spurn the notion of absolute truth and so leave every issue in life open for negotiation. This kind of thinking has wreaked havoc in society.

Jesus came to give us abundant life, but so many of us live defeated, stressed out, lonely, fearful lives. The problem is that we have believed a lie, one of any number of lies in Satan's arsenal. Oh, we don't have to believe all of his lies; in fact, many of us would probably pride ourselves on *not* believing many of his lies. But there may be just *one,* just one little lie hanging like a luscious piece of fruit, one little lie that we have picked and eaten. Perhaps we didn't see that it was a lie at first. Perhaps we just didn't take the time to see the consequences because it looked so innocent, even helpful. In any case, that one lie has placed us in bondage and has kept us from living the joyous, confident, and radiant life Christ offers.

If you are experiencing bondage in any area of your life, I pray that this book will give you the necessary tools to understand what lie(s) you have believed and what truth you need to discover from God's Word to replace that lie. I hope that you will understand that not one of Satan's lies is harmless. We cannot dwell on Satan's lies and come away unaffected. We need to be able to discern those lies when we hear them, to counter them with the Truth, and to help others to do the same.

Note from Nancy

"I'm not talking about a magic formula that will make problems vanish; I'm not offering any shortcuts to an easy life, nor am I promising the absence of pain and difficulties. Life is hard—there's no way around that. But I am talking about walking through the realities of life—things like rejection, loss, disappointment, wounds, and even death—in freedom and true joy" (p. 19).

Exploring the Truth . . .

Day One
The Power of the Truth (pp. 15–24)*

Realize

1. Read John 10:10. As you think about your life, would you say you are experiencing the abundant life Jesus came to give? Or do you find yourself just existing, coping, surviving, or struggling along? Explain.

   _____

   _____

Reflect

2. Look at the list of words on page 17 of *Lies Women Believe*. List below any of those words that describe your current season of life. Add other words of your own, if needed. (If you are not currently dealing with these kinds of feelings but you know someone who is, describe how you think she is feeling. You can use this study to learn how to help her and others who are struggling.)

   _____

   _____

3. Look at the list of words on page 19 of *Lies Women Believe*. Write below the words (or any of your own) that you would like to describe your life.

   _____

   _____

4. Read John 8:31–36. What do you think Jesus meant when He talked about being free? How do you know He did not mean being free to do anything we want to do?

   _____

   _____

5. Read Galatians 5:1 and John 14:6. What (*Who*) is the Truth that sets us free?

   _____

Respond

6. The young woman whose story begins on the bottom of page 21 said she had "given up hope" that she could ever be completely free from the moral habit that had kept her in

*Unless otherwise indicated, page numbers correspond to pages in *Lies Women Believe.*

bondage for years. Is there any area of your life where you have given up hope that you can ever be free?

To be free from the fear of man; to stop being so earthbound
_&_

7. In what ways would you like your life to change as a result of this study?

To be completely dependent on Jesus Christ; to fear
Him alone; to be able to trust Him with my future

Lord, I do want to experience growth as a result of this study. I pray that You will show me where I am in bondage and reveal to me any lies I may believe that are holding me there. Show me the Truth that I need to know so I can be truly free. Amen.

Day Two

Knowing Your Enemy, pp. 27–32

Realize

1. What do the following verses tell you about Satan and the way he operates?

- John 8:44

- 2 Corinthians 4:4

- 2 Corinthians 11:14

- Ephesians 6:11–12

- 1 Peter 5:8

Note from Nancy

"Regardless of the immediate source, anytime we receive input that is not consistent with the Word of God we can be sure Satan is trying to deceive and destroy us. What we read or hear may sound right, may feel right, may seem right—but if it is contrary to the Word of God, it isn't right" (p. 32).

Reflect

2. Why do Satan's lies often appear good and attractive?

_____

_____

3. What are some of the forms Satan's deception takes in our culture?

_____

_____

4. How can you discern the difference between Truth and deception? How can you keep from being deceived by Satan's lies?

_____

_____

_____

Respond

5. Satan knows that you will be more vulnerable to deception if you are not regularly meditating on God's Word. What "good" things keep you away from consistent study of the Word?

_____

_____

6. How can you raise your awareness of the Enemy? What can you do today to consciously embrace God's powerful Truth?

_____

_____

Lord, I know that Satan is a very real enemy and that he would like nothing better than to make me ineffective for You and Your kingdom. I ask that You will help me to stay in Your Word and to be aware of the truth that no matter how powerful Satan is, You are more powerful. Amen.

Day Three

Opening Your Eyes, pp. 32–36

Realize

1. Read Genesis 2:15–17 and 3:1–13. What seemingly good thing did Satan offer to Eve? Why did she think it was a good offer?

He offered fruit from the tree of knowledge of good + evil she saw it was good food, delight to the eyes, + would make her wise

Reflect

2. Make a list of the primary sources of input you have coming into your life (e.g., movies, books, certain friends, a counselor).

   Movies, magazines, friends, news

   _____

3. How careful are you about evaluating that input and seeking to discern Truth from error? Check the statement below that best describes you:

   ___ I have been heavily influenced by the culture and other "voices" around me and don't generally stop to evaluate what I hear and see in light of God's Word. I am not very discerning when it comes to Truth and error. (If this is really true of you, chances are you have been deceived and may not even realize that it describes you!)

   ✓ I am careful in some areas but not in others. I need to grow in spiritual discernment.

   ___ I evaluate the things I hear and see through the grid of God's Word and carefully consider the consequences when tempted with wrong choices. (According to Hebrews 5:14, the ability to discern between good and evil is a mark of spiritual maturity.)

4. Describe a time when you made a wrong choice without stopping to consider the cost and the consequences.

   _____

   _____

5. Identify the lie that Satan used to lead you to believe that you (or others) would not be affected by the sin.

   _____

   _____

6. What truth from God's Word can you now cite that would have helped you walk away from Satan's lie?

   _____

   _____

Respond

7. Ask God to help you grow in your ability to discern good from evil and to make godly choices. Ask Him to show you if there is any area of your life where you are currently being deceived by input that is contrary to the Word of God.

"Most people mindlessly accept whatever they hear and see. . . . Few Christians seriously consider the consequences of their choices. We simply live our lives, responding to the people, circumstances, and influences around us. . . . It all looks so good; it feels so right; it seems so innocent. But we end up in abusive relationships, head over heels in debt, angry, frustrated, trapped, and overwhelmed. We have been deceived" (p. 36).

Father, open my eyes so that I will not be deceived by Satan's lies.

Sometimes a course of action seems right when I don't stop to think about

Your Truth or about the consequences that could result. Teach me to

consider my choices in light of Your Word. Amen.

Day Four

Seeing the Progression, pp. 37–40

Realize

1. From pages 37–39 in *Lies Women Believe,* what are the four steps that take us from initial deception to bondage?

    1. Listening to things that are not true

    2. Dwell on the lie, if we allow our minds & hearts to dwell on things not true, sooner or later we...

    3. Believe the lie

    4. Act on the lie

2. Look again at Genesis 3:1–13. What did Eve do that matched each of these four steps that led her from deception to bondage?

    1.

    2.

    3.

    4.

Reflect

3. As long as we live in this world, we cannot completely isolate ourselves so that we never hear any lies. What is the difference between "hearing" and "listening to" lies?

Listening is active, intentional
Hearing is not actively involved, but more
perepheral.

4. Read Philippians 4:8–9. Why is it so important to be selective about the input we allow to come into our minds and to consciously choose to expose ourselves and listen to the Truth?

First God commands it. 2nd because what we listen to, becomes
our thinking + eventually leads to action

Respond

5. Review the list you made on Day Three of sources of input that you are allowing to come into your life. Is there anything on that list that is exposing you unnecessarily to deception?

Movies

6. What steps can you take to better protect your mind and heart from Satan's deception?

choose better movies

Lord, please show me any ways that I have made myself more vulnerable to
Satan's lies by the kinds of influences I am choosing to allow into my life.
Help me to fill my mind and heart with the Truth. Amen.

Day Five

Claiming the Truth, pp. 40–42

Realize

1. What are the three steps that will help us move from spiritual bondage to freedom?

1. _Identify the area of bondage or sinful behavior_
2. _Identify the lie at the root of that bondage or behavior_
3. _Replace the lie with the Truth._

Note from Nancy

"There are no harmless lies. We cannot expose ourselves to the world's false, deceptive way of thinking and come out unscathed" (p. 38).

" whatever is true, honorable, right, pure, lovely, good repute, excellent "

Note from Nancy

"Satan is a powerful enemy. His primary weapon is deception. His lies are powerful. But there is something even more powerful than Satan's lies—and that is the Truth" (pp. 41–42).

Reflect

2. How does the Truth counter lies?

   By listening, meditating, believing & acting on Truth instead of dwelling on lies

3. What does the Bible say about Truth in the following verses?

   • Psalm 33:4

   _____

   • Psalm 51:6

   _____

   • John 8:32

   _____

   • John 17:17

   _____

   • 2 Timothy 2:15

   _____

4. Read John 14:15–17 and 16:13. What is the Holy Spirit's role in helping us discern and walk in the Truth?

   _____

   _____

Respond

5. Can you identify any specific area(s) of bondage in your life—any area where you are not walking in freedom? (See pp. 17, 18, 41 in *Lies Women Believe* for examples of common types of bondage.)

   _____

   _____

6. "Every area of bondage in our lives can be traced back to a lie" (p. 40). Ask God to help you during the course of this study to discover what lie(s) you have believed that may have placed you in bondage. Also ask the Lord to show you the truth from His Word that counters Satan's lie.

Lord, I pray that You will show me clearly what lies I have believed. Then show me the Truth that will set me free. Thank You for Your Word and for Your Holy Spirit that point me to the Truth. Help me to claim Your Truth and to walk in Your Truth today and every day. Amen.

Walking Together in the Truth . . .

1. Why is our understanding of Truth so important?

   _____

   _____

2. A popular theme in our culture is that there are no absolutes. "All truth is good. Whatever truth works for you is good for you, and what works for me is good for me." While on the surface that appears very tolerant, where does this kind of thinking ultimately lead?

   _____

   _____

3. Describe some lies that are widely accepted as truth by our society. In what ways do these lies influence people's choices, and in what ways are they destructive to people's lives?

   _____

   _____

4. List three or four widespread problems in our world, and discuss how each could be the result of deception.

   _____

   _____

   _____

   _____

5. What women can you think of in the Scripture who were deceived and then influenced others to sin?

   _____

   _____

6. Discuss some ways women in our day have been deceived. How has that deception influenced sinful choices in others?

   _____

   _____

Note from Nancy

"From that moment [in the Garden of Eden] to this, Satan has used deception to win our affections, influence our choices, and destroy our lives. In one way or another, every problem we have in this world is the fruit of deception—the result of believing something that simply isn't true" (p. 32).

7. Share one or more ways that you have opened yourself up to deception in the past by choosing to expose yourself to input that is contrary to the Truth.

   _____

   _____

8. What are some illustrations of Satan's offers that women today find appealing? (Keep in mind that the things Satan tempts us with are not always inherently evil. The fruit that Eve ate wasn't bad or sinful in and of itself—in fact, it was something God had created. What made Eve's choice sinful was that God had said not to eat the fruit.)

   _____

   _____

9. Share a choice you were tempted to make that looked appealing and seemed right, but was contrary to God's Word. If you fell for the lie, describe any negative consequences that resulted.

   _____

   _____

10. Read together Acts 17:10–12. What did the people in Berea do in order to discern the Truth? How can we avoid being deceived and become more discerning about the input we receive?

    _____

    _____

CHAPTER
2

Trusting God

In a Nutshell . . .

Chapter 2 discusses six lies that many women wrestle with as they work through their perceptions of God. In a very real sense, whatever lies people believe about God will affect how they approach everything else in life. For example, if we doubt God's ultimate goodness, then we will be prone to discouragement and bitterness and will justify disobeying God's Word. Clearly, what we believe about God affects our outlook on everything else.

The first lie focuses on questioning God's goodness. The Bible tells us that God is good; however, in a world filled with hatred and evil, we may question if a good God could possibly be in control. Even if we can bring ourselves to agree that God is good, we might doubt that He is good *to us*, because our circumstances just don't bear that out. We need to acknowledge that God is completely good and that everything He does is good. Yes, human sin has given birth to enormous evil in the world. God is so powerful, however, that He is able to bring good results even out of evil circumstances.

The second lie concerns God's love. Many women don't believe that God could possibly love them. Though they may intellectually know of God's love, their feelings contradict what they know. They don't *feel* loved, so they don't believe that they *are* loved. At such times we need to move beyond our feelings and focus on the fact of God's love for us—a love so intense that He gave His Son to die for us.

The third lie addresses a hurdle that some women simply cannot cross. They cannot envision God as their loving Father because their earthly fathers were so unloving—demanding, abusive, absent, or critical. These women need to understand that God is not like any human they have ever known. He is perfect and perfectly good and loving.

The fourth lie runs rampant in our society. It is the lie that God is not enough. Society doesn't phrase it that way; instead, it tells us of all the things we must have in order to be complete, happy, and fulfilled. In reality, though, when we have God, we have all we really need.

Fifth is the lie that if we live God's way, we will be miserable. Many people think of God's commands as being a burden rather than a blessing. The Bible makes it clear, however, that Jesus came to set people free. The Bible gives guidance and instruction that, when obeyed, result in great blessing and protection. In fact, we disobey at our own peril. True freedom is found in obedience.

Finally, a sixth lie that many women believe about God is that He should fix all their problems. If they have God, then they should have problem-free lives, right? Wrong. God never promised to make life easy. He does promise, however, to walk through life with us, using the problems that come our way to mold us and shape us into the image of His Son.

Exploring the Truth . . .

Day One

God Is Good, pp. 45–49

Realize

1. When you were a child, you may have prayed this little rhyme before meals: "God is great, God is good . . ." Suppose you had never been to church and had never read a Bible. Would you think that a good God exists? Why or why not?

   In some ways yes because of the beauty of the world he created. But also no because of the evil + misery that happens even to "good" people

2. Look up Ephesians 1:3–14. Make a list of all the blessings God has given you that you can find in this passage.

   Blessed w/ every spiritual blessing, chose us in Him, to be holy + blameless, predestined to adoption, freely bestowed grace, in Him we have redemption, forgiveness of our tresspasses, grace lavished upon us, made known mystery of his will, obtained an inheritance sealed with the Holy spirit

3. According to Psalms 34:8 and 106:1, what are appropriate responses to the goodness of God?

   "Taste + see that the Lord is good; how blessed is the man who takes refuge in Him"
   "Praise the Lord, Give thanks to the Lord for He is good for His loving kindness is everlasting"

Reflect

4. Describe a situation, either past or present, in which you have been tempted to question God's goodness. (This could be anything from a difficult marriage to an unanswered prayer to an unexpected illness.)

Why did God not allow us to have more kids by changing Jeff's mind. I've doubted God's goodness when I think he withholds what I thought would have been good.

5. Romans 8:28 is a familiar verse to many believers. Read that verse as well as verses 29–39. What perspective about God and His good purposes does this passage provide to help us face painful or difficult life situations?

God doesn't just know us now, but "foreknew" + "predestined" us to become conformed to his image. He knew before we were that we are called according to his purposes. God doesn't make mistakes.

Respond

6. For whatever difficulties you are currently facing, choose to "give thanks to the Lord, for he is good," and to claim the promise of Romans 8:28–29. "Lord, even though I am facing difficulty regarding _____ , I know You are good, and You have promised to work that situation out for good. I know that Your commitment is to make me like Jesus. Thank You that You will use this circumstance (or person) as a means to fulfill Your good purpose for my life."

Lord, I know that You are good, but I admit that deep down I sometimes wonder about Your goodness when I'm facing hard times. Help me to trust in Your goodness, even when I cannot see it clearly. Amen.

Day Two

God Is Loving, pp. 50–54

Realize

1. Based on John 15:13, how did Jesus show His love for you? What else does the Bible tell you about God's love? (See John 3:16; Romans 5:8; 1 John 4:7–10.)

Jesus laid down His life for us   "God demonstrates his own love toward us in that while we were yet sinners, Christ died for us"

"love is from God, God is love

"In this is love, not that we loved God, but that He loved us + sent His son to be the propitiation for our sins"

Note from Nancy

"Theologically, intellectually, we know that God is good. But deep in many of our hearts, there lurks a suspicion that He may not really be good—at least, that He has not been good to me" (p. 48).

2. What effect do your feelings have on the truth of God's love for you?

my feelings can distort the truth, but also my dwelling on the truth of God's love can change + impact my feelings.

Reflect

3. Even though you may know that God loves you, you probably don't always *feel* that He does. What are some of the things that can cause you to *feel* that no one really loves or cares about you?

When I allow my "hurt feelings" to corrupt my feelings about people.

4. How can you live within the reality of God's love even on those days when you don't *feel* His love?

dwell on truth, remember God loved so much to send his son. Think about what is truth, use my mind not emotions

Respond

5. It has been said that if we could begin to grasp the greatness of God's love, our lives would be totally transformed. How would you think differently about God, about yourself, and about your circumstances if you truly understood how incredibly much God loves you?

I would trust him more, I would not be so quick to anger + bitterness + complaining if I remember howmuch God loves me. How could I be so complaining.

6. What are some ways you can grow in your understanding of the love of God?

focus, meditate, think on the ways God manifests his love to me

7. Read Paul's prayer in Ephesians 3:14–19. Personalize this prayer and pray it for yourself or for someone you know who has difficulty accepting the love of God.

_____

_____

_____

Lord, I know that You love me. I admit that on some days I just don't feel it.
Remind me at those times not to trust my feelings but to believe
the truths I know from Your Word. Amen.

Day Three

God Is Enough, pp. 54–55

Realize

1. Think about some of the advertisements and commercials you have seen recently. What are some of the things our culture tells us we must have in order to be truly fulfilled, happy, and complete?

   good looks, good health, fabulous home, stuff etc...

2. Read Colossians 2:9–10. What does it mean that you have been given "fullness" or "completeness" in Christ?

   "For in Him all the fulness of Deity dwells in bodily form, and in Him you have been made complete, + He is the head over all rule + authority" made complete – lacking nothing, needing nothing else

Reflect

3. Do you really believe that if you have God, you have enough? What are some of the "pluses" that you tend to think you have to have to be happy?

   More house, more enjoyment in life, more kids, more to do than just what I do,

4. What are some practical ways we can wean ourselves from dependence on earthly, temporal things and find full satisfaction in the Lord?

   Spend more time in Word + prayer, simple but it's doing it. The more my mind thinks on + meditates on God + the things of God The less discontent + "needy" I am

Respond

5. Read Psalm 73:23–26. Personalize the psalmist's prayer and write it in your own words. Ask God to make this prayer the true expression of your heart.

   I am with the Lord always, and you guide me in all things. Who is better than the Lord in heaven or earth? nothing. and I desire only you, Even if I fail, my weak frame gives out, you will remain my strength + all I need always.

> *Father, I am so prone to look to people and things other than You to fill the empty places of my heart and to satisfy my needs and longings. Your Word tells me that when I have You, I am complete. Thank You that no matter what else I may or may not have in this life, with You I have enough. Amen.*

Note from Nancy

> *"Do we really believe He is all we need? . . . Sure, I need God. But I need Him plus close friends . . . plus good health . . . plus a husband . . . plus children . . . plus a job that pays enough . . . plus . . ."* (p. 54).

Day Four

The Law of Liberty, pp. 55–56

Realize

1. What would the world be like if there were no laws? In what ways are laws necessary and beneficial to a society?

   There would be chaos and only the powerful/strong pnits would gain anything. Laws insure justice, organization, safety, equality.

2. What does Deuteronomy 6:24–25 say about the value and blessing of obedience to God's laws?

   "to fear the Lord our God for our good always + for our survival
   "it will be righteousness for us if we are careful to observe all his commandments

Reflect

3. Read James 1:19–27. What does James mean when he refers to "the perfect law that gives freedom" (v. 25)? How do God's laws give us freedom?

   They give us boundaries to do what God says is best; It keeps us from the danger do doing anything we want

4. Describe a time when you decided to do your own thing instead of obeying God. What happened?

5. In what ways are God's restrictions actually a benefit and a blessing to His children? How could you explain their benefit to others?

   Keeps us out of sin & its consequences, keeps relationship better both w/ God + others; remember He is all wisdom, how can we even think we know better than him.

Respond

6. Are there any biblical commands you have been resisting or hesitating to obey, thinking you would be better off doing things your way? "Obedience is the pathway to freedom." Will you surrender and choose to obey God's way?

   Probably my role as a submissive wife giving everything to God, my thoughts,

Lord, I know that the direction in Your Word has been given to us out of love. Help me to trust You and to be willing to obey You even when Your ways do not make sense to my finite mind. Amen.

Day Five

Divine Delays and Denials, pp. 56–58

Realize

1. What are some illustrations of the way our society is conditioned to expect quick fixes?

   Take a pill, lose weight - Marriage unhappy, get divorced. Unfulfilled, buy something;

2. Read 2 Corinthians 12:7–10. What kind of problem was Paul facing? What do you think his motivation was in asking for it to be removed? Do you think he was wrong to pray this way?

   Some "thorn", trouble, causing pain or difficulty. He wanted to be free from the trouble. No it wasn't wrong to ask, but he also knew when to stop asking... only 3 times.

3. What was God's response to Paul's request?

   God said "my grace is sufficient for you" I need to be exalted in you, not exalting yourself.

Reflect

4. What difficulties are you facing today? Are there problems and trials in your life that you've asked God to remove and He has not?

   Jealousy

5. Why might God sometimes choose *not* to fix or remove your problems? What greater goals might He have in mind? If God chooses not to remove your difficulties, what does the Bible tell you that He may be trying to do instead (Job 23:10; Romans 5:3–4; James 1:2–4)?

   Strengthen my faith, bring perseverance, character those, testing produces endurance that we may be found perfect + complete, lacking nothing

6. In what ways have you seen God work through difficulties in your life or in others' lives?

Respond

7. Identify the biggest problem you are facing currently. What do you think God may want to teach you through your current struggle?

Note from Nancy

"The Truth is, life is hard. We live in a fallen world. Even those who have been redeemed live in earthly bodies and have to deal with the realities of temptation, sin (both our own and others'), disease, loss, pain, and death. . . . God is not removed or detached from our problems. . . . He uses pressures and problems to mold and shape our lives and to make us like His Son Jesus" (p. 58).

If God never "fixed" that problem, how could He use this circumstance to change you and to reveal His character through you?

letting my kids go + continuing to teach them

Lord, I know that You want what is best for me. You desire to help me become mature. I understand that sometimes the only way I will grow is through pain. In the difficulties that I am facing today, Lord, I pray that You will grant me peace and patience to accept Your perfect will in my life. Amen.

Walking Together in the Truth . . .

1. Why is our view of God so important?

2. What are some faulty views people have of God? How do those views affect the way people live?

3. In your reading and study of chapter 2, what truth about God did you find particularly encouraging or helpful? (See page 59 in *Lies Women Believe*.)

   God is good + God is enough

Lie: God is not really good. If He were, He would . . .

Truth: God is good, and everything He does is good. He never makes mistakes.

4. What is the source of all evil in the world? Read Genesis 3:1–8, and discuss how sin has affected all people and all creation.

   Sin. No one is good. Thus nothing they do is truly, godly good w/out the spirit. After the fall God not only cursed Adam but also cursed the ground too. All creation groans under the weight do sin

5. In response to the sin that brought evil into our world, what did God do for us? Read and discuss Ephesians 2:4–10.

made us alive together w/ christ

Note from Nancy

"The Truth is, God is good. Whether or not His choices seem good to us, He is good. Whether or not we feel it, He is good. Whether or not it seems true in my life or yours, He is still good" (pp. 48–49).

Lie: God doesn't love me.

Truth: God's love for me is infinite and unconditional. I don't have to perform to earn God's love or favor. He always has my best interests at heart.

Lie: God is just like my father.

Truth: God is exactly what He has revealed Himself to be in His Word. He is infinitely more wise and loving than any earthly father could ever be.

6. Why do people often feel that they need to earn God's love? What part do earthly fathers sometimes play in this understanding?

7. Read Romans 8:35–39. How does Paul describe the love of God? What does it mean to you to be loved in this way?

Nothing can seperate us from the Love of God

Note from Nancy

"God loves me . . . because He is love. His love for me is not based on anything I have ever done or ever could do for Him. It is not based on my performance. I do not deserve His love and could never earn it" (p. 51).

Lie: God is not really enough.

Truth: God is enough. If I have Him, I have all I need.

8. What are some of the things you tend to think you need to fill the empty places of your heart?

Better relationships, more kids, bigger house, more room, more "time off" more understanding mate

9. How might we live differently if we really believed that Christ and His Word were sufficient to meet the deepest needs of our hearts?

would live in true contentment whatever came, knowing its all from God & His will. Live selflessly with an eye always toward heaven holding very loosely to things of this earth.

Lie: God's ways are too restrictive.

Truth: God's ways are best, and his restrictions are for my good. Resisting or rebelling will only bring trouble.

10. What are some instructions in the New Testament that some people would think are burdensome, unreasonable, or unfair? Discuss how those instructions are actually for our good and our protection.

To take up cross, to be willing to die to self totally

Lie: God should fix my problems.

Truth: Life is hard. God doesn't guarantee that He will fix all my problems; in fact, God is more concerned about fulfilling His eternal purpose in and through me in the midst of those problems.

Note from Nancy

"We want God to fix all our problems. God says instead, 'I have a purpose for your problems. I want to use your problems to change you and to reveal My grace and power to the world.' That is the Truth—and the Truth will set you free" (p. 58).

11. In what ways does God work through our problems to help us mature in Him? Have you ever experienced this kind of growth through pain?

12. Commentator G. Campbell Morgan wrote, "The supreme need in every hour of difficulty and distress is for a fresh vision of God. Seeing Him, all else takes on proper perspective and proportion." What is one area of your life that would be different if you were to get a "fresh vision of God"?

Seeing Myself as God Sees Me

In a Nutshell . . .

Chapter 3 discusses six lies that many women believe about themselves. The previous chapter discussed lies women believe about God and explained how what we believe about God affects what we believe about everything else. One crucial area affected is our beliefs about ourselves. If we don't believe that God is good, loving, compassionate, and forgiving, then we won't be able to believe that He has our best in mind, that He loves us, that He understands us, and that He can forgive even our deepest, darkest sins.

The first lie many women believe about themselves relates to their worth. Many women feel inferior and worthless. The problem arises when women allow others to decide their value instead of accepting the Truth that, if they are in Christ, they are dearly loved children of God.

The second lie is rooted in our culture. Many people try to tell us that we need to "love ourselves," and that will solve all our problems. The problem is that we already *do* love ourselves. That comes naturally. What often appears as a lack of self-love is actually a faulty view of God and our value to Him. Women need to learn to receive God's love, so His love can fill us and then overflow to others.

The third lie is found in those self-fulfilling words, "I can't help the way I am." We have built a nation full of victims—whenever someone does something wrong, it's usually someone else's fault. While our circumstances do indeed shape us, we are responsible for the choices we make. As believers, the Holy Spirit lives in us and gives us the power to obey God.

The fourth lie also comes from our culture. We live in a nation of people clamoring for their "rights." When we focus on our perceived "rights," we are setting ourselves up for disappointment and hurt. True freedom comes when we relinquish our "rights" and expectations to God.

Fifth is the lie about physical beauty. Many women look at magazine covers and long for such clear skin, such smooth thighs, such a flat stomach, such a perfect nose. The billions of dollars women spend every year trying to look young or become beautiful attest to the power of this lie. While there's nothing wrong with being physically attractive, Christian women ought to be more concerned about cultivating true, inner beauty of the spirit—the kind of beauty that increases rather than diminishes with age.

The last lie focuses on our deep, personal longings. Like the lie about "rights," many women feel that God owes them the fulfillment of their deepest longings. While the longings themselves may not be sinful, the danger is that we will begin to demand that God meet our expectations or that we will seek to meet our desires in sinful ways. By focusing on our unfulfilled longings, we can miss the fact that God by His very presence fulfills our deepest needs. He promises that one day we will lack nothing.

Exploring the Truth . . .

Day One

Accepting God's Assessment, pp. 63–71

Realize

1. Describe a time in your life when you felt on top of the world. Next, describe a time when you felt completely worthless. What common factors do you find in both experiences? (For example, were your feelings dependent on others' responses to you, on how you looked, on how you performed?)

_____

_____

2. Read Psalm 139:1–18. What do you learn from this psalm about God's heart and thoughts toward you?

_____

_____

Reflect

3. Is there someone whose affirmation you crave? Someone whose approval matters more to you than God's?

_____

_____

4. How has that longing for human acceptance affected your thoughts? Your emotions? Your behavior? Your relationships with others?

____I keep distant from really getting close w/ people
I'm pretty surface oriented_____

5. Read Romans 5:6–11. What makes it possible for us, as fallen sinners and enemies of God, to be accepted by God?

_____

_____

6. What effect do you think a renewed vision of your position in Christ might have on your interactions with family and friends?

_____

_____

Respond

7. How can you begin to renew your mind, to understand and trust God's love for you and His acceptance of you through Christ?

meditate on Christ's gift, on what God did
for me, on how precious I am to Him

Lord, thank You for loving me so much. Thank You for choosing me and saving me.
Thank You that through Christ I have been made acceptable to You and that I am
Your treasured possession. Help me to think of myself as Your beloved daughter
and to rejoice in the privilege of my relationship with You. Amen.

Day Two

Accepting Responsibility, pp. 71–73

Realize

1. List some of the excuses you've heard people use to explain their wrong behavior (e.g., "My parents got divorced"; "We never had much money"; "I never felt loved").

I had a bad childhood, my husband doesn't show love,
I'm tired; I've had a bad day

2. Obviously, our upbringing and environment have an effect on who we are. However, these factors cannot *determine* who we are. Negative circumstances don't always mean that a child will turn out badly, nor do positive experiences always mean that a child will turn out good. What do you think makes the difference?

Our response to the experiences & what we choose to
do with it.

Note from Nancy

"This lie—'I can't help the way I am'—makes us into helpless victims of other people and outside circumstances. The suggestion is that someone or something else is responsible for who we are. . . . We somehow believe that we are destined to be controlled by whoever or whatever is pulling our strings" (p. 73).

3. Some people live as victims all their lives. What effect does it have on them? Who controls their lives?

   They live w/out responsibility for their own actions + who they are. They blame everyone/thing else. Outside influences direct them instead of God.

Reflect

4. Read Colossians 3:1–17. On the basis of who Christ is and what He has done for us (Colossians 1—2), the apostle Paul tells us that we are responsible to make godly choices in every area of life, including our attitudes, our behavior, and our relationships. What are we to "put off"? What are we to "put on"?

   Put off: anger, wrath, malice slander, abusive speech, lying
   Put on: compassion, kindness, humility, gentleness, patience, bearing + forgiving one another, love

5. In Galatians 5:22–23, what does Paul promise that the Holy Spirit will help to do in our lives?

   The fruit of the spirit is love, joy peace, patience, kindness, goodness, faithfulness, gentleness + self control

Respond

6. In what area(s) of your life have you been blaming your circumstances, your upbringing, or another person for the way you are, rather than assuming personal responsibility? How do you think God wants you to view that struggle? What fruit of the Spirit do you need to help you deal with the issue?

   I get frustrated + sometimes depressed when things don't get done around the house + I blame Jeff, or busyness, or errands or other stuff instead of using patience + humility

Lord, I agree with You that I am not a helpless victim of my circumstances or my past. I understand that I may not be able to change the circumstances of my life, but, because of what Jesus has done for me and in me, I can control my attitude and my responses. By the power of Your Spirit help me to choose to obey You, to take responsibility for my actions, and to be changed into the image of Christ. Amen.

Day Three

Yielding Rights, pp. 73–76

Realize

1. Look at the list of things that many women claim as their "rights" on page 75 of *Lies Women Believe*. While you might wish all of these things to be true in your own life, what makes it inaccurate to claim them as your rights?

_____

_____

2. When people claim their rights, how do they respond when those supposed rights are violated? Why does claiming rights so often result in anger, bitterness, depression, and broken relationships?

They protest, get angry, demand their way _____

_____

Reflect

3. Read Psalm 37:1–11. What are the attitudes and behaviors of a person who is claiming her rights? What are the attitudes and responses of the person who has yielded her rights and expectations to God?

She trusts in the Lord, cultivates faithfulness, delights in the Lord, rests + waits on the Lord

Note from Nancy

"Women have been told that demanding their rights was the ticket to happiness and freedom. . . . The fact is, successful relationships and healthy cultures are not built on the claiming of rights but on the yielding of rights" (p. 74).

4. In what area(s) of your life have you tended to think that something is your "right" when it may not truly be a "right" at all (e.g., you might think you have a "right" to a healthy marriage, good children, a problem-free church, faithful friends, etc.)?

I think the only thing I might think I have a right to is help with household chores & having Jeff put me + my "to do" list before others

Respond

5. Make a list of any "rights" you may still be holding on to, along with any expectations you have placed on others. Consciously surrender each of those "rights" and expectations to God.

_____

_____

Father, I confess my tendency to defend my "rights" and to become angry, resentful, or impatient when those "rights" are violated. By faith, I yield all those "rights" and expectations to You and trust You to meet my needs and to work out Your purposes for my life. Amen.

Day Four

Lasting Beauty, pp. 77–82

Realize

1. Some of the most physically beautiful women are also extremely miserable. Why doesn't physical beauty necessarily make a woman happy?

Because anything outside to God won't satisfy

2. Read 1 Samuel 16:7. What does it mean that God looks at people's hearts?

God knows the attitudes, emotions beliefs, values etc the real you, not who you pretend to be or try to be on the outside.

Reflect

3. How would you compare the time and effort you invest in your physical appearance with the time and effort you put into developing a beautiful heart and spirit?

I spend more time in my exercise, dressing, painting my nails etc than in reading his word etc. But how do I develop a beautiful heart & spirit. "By obedience

Note from Nancy

"The deception that physical beauty is to be esteemed above beauty of heart, spirit, and life leaves both men and women feeling unattractive, ashamed, embarrassed, and hopelessly flawed. . . . God's Word tells us the Truth about the transitory nature of physical beauty and the importance of pursuing lasting, inner beauty" (pp. 78–79).

4. Read Proverbs 31:30; 1 Timothy 2:9–10; and 1 Peter 3:1–6. Why is it a shortsighted mistake for us to become preoccupied with external, physical beauty?

Because its not lasting & if we focus on external we neglect the internal lasting beauty

5. According to the passages above, what are the qualities that make a woman truly beautiful to God and to others? How do those qualities affect her outer appearance?

Chaste + respectful, gentle + quiet spirit, submissive to husbands, doing what is right w/out fear, modest + descreet attire, good works

6. If God were to hold a mirror up to your heart today, what would He see?

One who desires to be more like Jesus, desires to love God more, desires to put God before myself. But I also know God sees many failings of those desires. Thinking too much about how I or my house look etc.

Respond

7. How can you develop a heart that reflects great beauty?

Father, I realize that the most important beauty I can have is the
kind that comes from within. Please develop in me that true,
enduring, inner beauty that is pleasing to You. Amen.

Day Five

Surrendering Our Longings, pp. 82–86

Realize

1. What are some of your heart's desires that have not yet been fulfilled (e.g., to get married, to improve your marriage, to have children, to regain health, etc.)?

   deep, deep love & desire for Jeff, more kids

2. Read Deuteronomy 8:3. Why did God allow His people to go hungry (i.e., to have unfulfilled longings) in the desert?

   to make them understand that man does not live by bread alone but by the word of God

3. What are some other reasons God might not allow all of His children's longings to be fulfilled here and now?

   So we would long for heaven + Him, so we would not worship anything other than God

Reflect

4. As you think about the legitimate longings you recorded in question 1 above, have you fallen into the trap of demanding that God fulfill your desires or resenting that He has not chosen to do so? Have you made any sinful choices as a result of trying to meet those longings in illegitimate ways?

   I've often wondered + complained why God has not answered but outside of talking to Jeff nothing else

5. From Ecclesiastes 3:11, what does it mean that God has placed eternity in your heart?

   There is a natural God given longing for God & heaven placed there by him that when called we will answer & be satisfied only by Him

Note from Nancy

"It is important to understand that our inner longings are not necessarily sinful in and of themselves. What is wrong is demanding that those longings be fulfilled here and now, or insisting on meeting those longings in illegitimate ways" (p. 85).

6. Read Philippians 3:20—4:1. What does it mean that your citizenship is in heaven? What implications do this passage and the verse from Ecclesiastes have as you face what may be legitimate longings that God has not chosen to fulfill?

_____

_____

7. According to Psalm 16:11, where is the only place that all our longings can be completely met?

_____

_____

Respond

8. Elisabeth Elliot reminds us that unfulfilled longings provide "material for sacrifice." What longings can you offer up as a sacrifice to the Lord?

_____

_____

Lord, I have many desires deep within me. I understand that my longings are not necessarily bad, but in my impatience, Lord, help me not to attempt to meet those longings in wrong ways. Help me to be patient, knowing that You know my longings and that You have my best in mind. Thank You that the day is coming when the deepest thirst and longings of my soul will be fully satisfied in Your presence. Amen.

Walking Together in the Truth . . .

1. In your reading and study of chapter 3, what truth did you find especially encouraging or helpful? (See page 87 in *Lies Women Believe*.) Did you find any of these truths difficult to accept?

_____

_____

Lie: I'm not worth anything.

Truth: My value is not determined by what others think of me or what I think of myself. My value is determined by how God views me—and I am precious to Him.

Lie: I need to learn to love myself.

Truth: By faith, I need to receive God's love for me. I naturally love myself; I need to deny myself and let God love others through me.

2. What criteria do most people use to evaluate their own worth or the worth of others?

    _____

    _____

3. We hear a lot about the need for positive self-esteem and the need to learn to love ourselves. What is the danger in this kind of focus?

    _____

    _____

4. Read together Luke 12:4–7. Why is it safe to fear God?

    _____

    _____

Lie: I can't help the way I am.

Truth: If I am God's child, I can choose to obey Him. I am responsible for my own choices. God's Spirit can change me.

5. Read Romans 6:1–14 and 8:1–2. According to these passages, why are we free to live a life of victory over sin and self? What is our source of power for living this new life?

    _____

    _____

6. As Paul acknowledges in Galatians 5:17, Christians are engaged in a battle between the flesh and the Spirit. What biblical counsel would you give to a believer who is struggling with sin and says, "I just can't change"? (See 2 Corinthians 5:17 and Galatians 5:16.)

    _____

    _____

Note from Nancy

"Satan knows that if we believe we can't help the way we are, we will never change. We will go on living in bondage. If we believe we are doomed to fail, to keep on sinning, or to be miserable, we will fail, we will keep on sinning, and we will always be unhappy, frustrated women" (p. 73).

Lie: I have my rights.

Truth: Claiming rights will put me in bondage. Yielding rights will set me free.

7. Give an illustration of a time when you claimed a right and responded sinfully when that right was violated (e.g., when you were stuck in traffic, when a family member wronged you, etc.).

_____

_____

8. How does yielding our rights affect our relationship with God? With others?

_____

_____

9. What is a right or an expectation you were challenged to surrender to the Lord during your study this week?

_____

_____

Lie: Physical beauty matters more than inner beauty.

Truth: Physical beauty is fleeting. The beauty that matters most to God is the beauty of my inner spirit and character.

Note from Nancy

"We as Christian women should seek to reflect the beauty, order, excellence, and grace of God through both our outward and inner person. . . . The outward appearance of the Christian woman is to reflect a heart that is simple, pure, and well-ordered. . . . In this way, she reflects the true condition of her heart and her relationship with the Lord, and she makes the gospel attractive to the world" (pp. 80–81).

10. Whom do you know who models the beauty of Christ in her spirit?

_____

_____

11. What are some practical ways that Christian women can cultivate true, spiritual beauty? How can Christian women make the gospel "attractive to the world"?

_____

_____

Lie: I should not have to live with unfulfilled longings.

Truth: I will always have unfulfilled longings this side of heaven. The deepest longings of my heart cannot be fulfilled by any person or thing. My unfulfilled longings can help me look forward to heaven.

12. Read Hebrews 11:13–16. What do these verses mean as they compare life on this earth to what has been promised to believers? How can a focus on eternity help us live with unfulfilled longings here on earth?

_____

_____

Understanding Sin

In a Nutshell . . .

Chapter 4 addresses lies women believe about sin. Many people would like to get rid of the notion of "sin" altogether. They believe that there is no absolute standard of right and wrong, that truth is a personal issue, depending on what's best for you, and that tolerance is the key for unity in our world. Those are nice thoughts; unfortunately, they're not true. A perfect God exists, and evil exists as well. The entire Bible tells the story of what God does about sin. Clearly, sin is real and important to God—so important, in fact, that He sent His Son to die, in order to deal with it once and for all.

The first lie says that people can sin and get away with it. That one seems so true to us, because it appears to happen all the time. In fact, we see people who actually seem to get rewards for their sin: money, fame, power, and promotions. However, the Truth is that sinners will ultimately receive the consequences of their sin. The pleasures that sin gives will eventually turn sour.

The second and third lies represent two ends of a spectrum. One lie is that our sin is no big deal; the other is that our sin is such a big deal that God Himself cannot even forgive it. Both are lies. According to God, all sin is sin, no matter how much we try to rationalize it. While different sins may have more or less severe consequences, any sin is still worthy of death because it is an act of rebellion against God. On the other hand, to believe that our sin is too much for God is to underestimate the power of the Cross.

The fourth lie spreads responsibility for sin on everyone else's shoulders but our own. We justify our sins all the time, blaming them on unhappy marriages, character traits we inherited from our parents, or results of our childhood experiences. The Truth is that we are responsible for every choice we make—including our choices to sin.

The last lie in this chapter deals with our attitude toward sin. As believers, we have been given the Holy Spirit and a brand new life. Even though we will struggle with our sinful flesh until the day we die, we must recognize that we are no longer in bondage to sin. We *can* experience victory over sin, because of what Christ has done for us.

Exploring the Truth . . .

Day One

The Truth About Sin, pp. 91–98

Realize

1. In your own words, define "sin."

_____

_____

2. Read Genesis 2:15—3:24. What did God provide for Adam and Eve? Why did God impose such severe consequences for eating a piece of fruit?

_____

_____

3. According to Romans 5:12 and 18a, what was the effect of their sin on the world?

_____

_____

Reflect

4. Even if no one ever finds out about your sin, Who *does* know? (See Proverbs 5:21; 20:27.) The fear of the Lord has been described as "living in the constant, conscious awareness of the presence of God." How could that awareness protect you from sin?

_____

_____

Note from Nancy

"Most people simply don't make the connection between their natural, fleshly choices and the consequences in their lives, their marriages, their children, their health, and their relationships with God and others" (p. 96).

5. You may not consciously believe that you can sin and get away with it. But we all live as if we believed this lie at times. Give an example of a sin you committed without really stopping to contemplate what it would cost you.

_____

_____

Respond

6. Becoming more conscious of the true consequences of sin will help protect us from sin. Based on the Scripture as well as your own experience, make a list of as many of sin's consequences as you can think of.

You may want to carry that list with you this week, so that when you are tempted to sin, you can remember the consequences before you make your choice.

_____

_____

Lord, I understand that sin is very real—so real, in fact, that You had to pay the price for my sin with the death of Jesus. Lord, You know everything about me: my thoughts, motives, and desires. Help me to be mindful of Your presence in every moment of my life today. Guard my heart and keep me from sin, for Jesus' sake. Amen.

Day Two

Seeing Sin for What It Is, pp. 98–100

Realize

1. Have you ever compared yourself to other people and thought, "At least I'm not *that* bad"? What sins in your life seem less important when compared to the sins in others' lives? (Be honest!)

_____

_____

2. Read Galatians 5:19–21. List the acts of the flesh. While different sins may have different consequences, are any of these sins "less sinful" than the others in God's eyes?

_____

_____

3. All sin has one ultimate consequence, according to Romans 6:23. What is the consequence?

_____

_____

> ## Note from Nancy
>
> *"Compared to others who commit these kinds of 'serious' sins, it's easy for us to feel that we aren't so bad. . . . We may not even consider them to be sins at all—preferring to think of them as weaknesses, struggles, or personality traits"* (p. 99).

Reflect

4. Throughout the Old Testament, why did God require blood sacrifices (Hebrews 9:22)? How did Jesus' death fulfill this requirement?

_____

_____

5. Considering the price Jesus paid for you, what effect should that realization have on how you view the "little" sins in your life?

_____

_____

Respond

6. What sin(s) in your life have you been trivializing or not taking really seriously? Ask God to give you a greater sense of the sinfulness of sin and what your sin cost Him.

_____

_____

Lord, I know that I am a sinner, and I confess that sometimes I forget that every sin I commit is an act of rebellion against You. There are no "little" sins, for they are all equally evil in Your eyes. I pray that You will help me not to excuse my sin but to realize its seriousness and to be truly repentant. Help me to see myself and my sin in the light of Your absolute holiness and the cross of Christ. Amen.

Day Three

Sin and Grace, pp. 100–102

Realize

1. Some people struggle with receiving God's forgiveness because they feel their sins are just too great. What types of sins do people tend to think are "too serious" for God to be able to forgive?

_____

_____

2. When Jesus died on the cross, what did He accomplish (Isaiah 53:6; John 1:29)?

_____

_____

Reflect

3. If we think that our sins are too big for God to forgive, what are we implying about Jesus' death on the cross?

_____

_____

4. According to Proverbs 28:13 and 1 John 1:9, how do we appropriate God's forgiveness? What is the result when we do?

_____

_____

5. What types of things do people do in an attempt to "do penance" for their sins? What are some of the ways you have tried to "earn" God's favor after you have sinned?

_____

_____

6. What would you say to someone who thinks that her sins are too big for God to forgive?

_____

_____

Note from Nancy

"[Many women] find it difficult to accept God's mercy and forgiveness. They feel that in order to be restored into favor and fellowship with God there is something further they must do to atone for their sin; that they must do 'penance'; that perhaps they can be good enough to make up for the wrong they have done " (p. 101).

Respond

7. What does God's forgiveness of your sins mean to you?

_____

_____

Father, I know that the blood of Christ is sufficient to cover all my sin.
Thank You for offering cleansing and forgiveness to every sinner who comes to
You in repentance and faith. Thank You that no sin is too big for You to forgive.
By faith, I receive Your forgiveness for every sin that I have ever committed.
Help me to walk as Your cleansed, forgiven child. Amen.

Day Four

Taking Responsibility, pp. 102–5

Realize

1. Read 1 John 1:5–10. What does it mean to "walk in the light" as it relates to our sin?

_____

_____

2. Second Corinthians 5:21 describes Jesus' sacrifice for our sin. What does this verse tell us about the great exchange that God made possible at Calvary?

_____

_____

Reflect

3. Are there sins in your life that you have been excusing as mere "weaknesses" or "personality traits"? If so, what are they?

_____

_____

Note from Nancy

"When we are angry, depressed, bitter, annoyed, impatient, or fearful, our natural response is to shift at least some of the responsibility on the people or circumstances that 'made' us that way" (p. 104).

4. Have you been playing the blame game? Are there sins you are committing that you have justified as a reaction to your circumstances or the failures of others (e.g., you blame your husband, your kids, your job, your upbringing)? If so, what are they?

_____

_____

5. Read Psalm 51:1–10. How did David find forgiveness and relief from guilt after he had sinned with Bathsheba?

_____

_____

Respond

6. Re-read Psalm 51:1–10 aloud, making it your prayer to God. Accept personal responsibility for any specific sins God has brought to your mind as you have answered these questions. Confess them to Him as sin. (*To confess* simply means to agree with God about your sin, to call it what He calls it—not a mistake, a problem, a struggle, or a justified reaction to someone else's sin—but *sin*.)

_____

_____

Lord, I acknowledge that I am fully responsible for my own actions
and choices, regardless of my circumstances or what has been done to me.
I know that at times I try to cover my sins by blaming other people or
circumstances. Forgive me, Lord. Thank You for Your grace that is
so abundant when I come to You as a guilty sinner. Amen.

Day Five

Victory over Sin, pp. 105–11

Realize

1. Salvation does not make us sinless. In fact, read about Paul's struggle with sin in Romans 7:15–25. In what ways do you resonate with Paul's words in this passage? According to verse 25, what is the key to experiencing victory over "the law of sin"?

_____

_____

2. Based on Romans 8:1–14, describe the role of the Holy Spirit in setting us free from slavery to the flesh.

_____

_____

Reflect

3. Do you feel in bondage to any sins in your life that you feel you just can't overcome?

_____

_____

4. How does Christ's work on the cross have the power to set us free from bondage to sin? What truths could you share with a friend who is being defeated by habitual sin?

_____

_____

Respond

5. Read Galatians 2:20. What does it mean to be crucified with Christ? How does that translate into how you will live today?

_____

_____

Note from Nancy

"The Truth is, you and I are powerless to change ourselves, for 'Apart from me,' Jesus said, 'you can do nothing' (John 15:5). So what are we to do? How can we be set free from habitual sin? It is the Truth that sets us free. The Truth is, through Christ's finished work on the cross, we can live in victory over sin . . . we no longer have to live as slaves to sin" (p. 108).

6. The first step to walking in victory over sin is to acknowledge that you do not have to live under sin's control (assuming you are a child of God). Talk with the Lord about the specific areas where you have continued to give in to sin's control. Thank Him that at the cross, Jesus broke the power of sin to rule your life. Ask Him to show you how to walk in submission to the Spirit and how to experience the victory that is yours through Christ.

Father, thank You for Jesus, who came to set me free from sin's bondage.
I agree with Your Word that I am no longer enslaved to sin. Help me to live in
that freedom. Thank You for Your Spirit, who lives within me and gives me
the power to say "no" to my flesh and "yes" to You. Amen.

Walking Together in the Truth . . .

1. In a sense, the problem of sin is the topic of the entire Bible: how sin began and what God chose to do about it because He loves us. Think about the character of God (His love, His justice, His power, etc.). Why does God take sin so seriously? Why couldn't He have said, "I forgive you, Adam and Eve. Let's just put this little fruit-eating episode behind us and move on"?

   _____

   _____

2. In your reading and study of chapter 4, what truth did you find especially encouraging or helpful? (See page 112 in *Lies Women Believe*.) Did you find any of these truths difficult to understand or accept?

   _____

   _____

Lie: I can sin and get away with it.

Truth: Sin has consequences, and I cannot escape those consequences.

3. Many people want to deny the reality of sin. However, the reality of sin has affected our world. How do the consequences listed on page 97 of *Lies Women Believe* manifest themselves in our society today? Does anyone really sin and "get away with it"?

   _____

   _____

4. Share about a situation in which you made a sinful choice ("big" or "small") and experienced consequences that you had not anticipated.

   _____

   _____

Lie: My sin isn't really that bad.

Truth: Every act of sin is an act of rebellion against God and required the death of His Son. No sin is small.

Lie: God can't forgive what I have done.

Truth: The blood of Jesus is sufficient to cover any and every sin. No sin is too big for God to forgive. God's grace is always greater than our sin.

5. These two lies—"My sin isn't really that bad" and "God can't forgive what I've done"—are opposite sides of the same coin. One trivializes sin; the other trivializes the grace of God. Both diminish Jesus' death on the cross, and both are lies that the Enemy uses to keep us in bondage. Share either (a) a sin in your life that you have tended to shrug off as "not that bad" or (b) a sin you have committed for which you have struggled to receive God's forgiveness.

    _____

    _____

6. How does the Cross show us the Truth about both of these lies?

    _____

    _____

Note from Nancy

"The Cross shows us in the starkest possible terms what God thinks of our sin; it reveals the incredible cost He paid to redeem us from those 'weaknesses' that we trivialize in our minds. The Cross also displays in brilliant Technicolor the love and mercy of God for even the 'chief of sinners'" (p. 101).

Lie: I am not fully responsible for my actions and reactions.

Truth: I am responsible for my own choices.

7. Read the quote on page 105 of *Lies Women Believe* that begins, "Sin is the best news there is . . ." What does the writer mean? In what sense is sin "good news"?

    _____

    _____

8. Describe an area where you have had the tendency to blame someone or something else for your sin, rather than taking personal responsibility for your own choices.

    _____

    _____

Lie: I cannot walk in consistent victory over sin.

Truth: I am not a slave to sin. I have been set free through Christ.

9. Why do you think God doesn't just zap us into sinless perfection the moment we receive Christ as Savior?

_____

_____

10. According to Hebrews 10:10, holiness is not something we *do*; it is something we *are* because of Christ. How should that truth affect how we live and how we deal with our tendency to sin?

_____

_____

Note from Nancy

"What about you, my friend? The Enemy wants to keep you in bondage to fear, doubt, and guilt. God wants you to walk in freedom, faith, and assurance of forgiveness. No matter how 'good' you may be, the only way you can ever be made right with God is through faith in Christ. And no matter how 'great' a sinner you may have been, His grace is sufficient for you. Through the death of Christ, God has made the only acceptable provision for your sin" (p. 110).

11. As children of God, we are free from sin's bondage, but our flesh still wars against the indwelling Spirit of God. What are some practical ways we can deal with our flesh and bring it under the Spirit's control every day?

_____

_____

12. What is one area of your life where you are not walking in victory over sin? Pray for each woman who shares. (As the Lord prompts, commit yourself to pray daily over the next week for one of the women who expresses a battle with a particular sin in her life. Pray that she will enter into the victory that is available to her through Christ.)

_____

_____

CHAPTER

5

Setting Priorities

In a Nutshell . . .

In this chapter, we will consider three lies that many women believe about their priorities. Then we will discover the corresponding truths in God's Word. Throughout this week, you will be encouraged to apply God's Truths to your personal priorities.

The first lie has to do with our many activities and involvements. Look around at the women you know—your friends, your sister, coworkers—or take a quick glance at your own schedule. In spite of countless timesaving devices and conveniences, most modern women (including Christian women) are living breathless, harried, frazzled lives and are believing that there just aren't enough hours in the day.

The second lie concerns the priority we place on our personal relationship with Christ. Perhaps we think we are just too busy to fit a quiet time into our schedule. Maybe "quiet" has become a long-lost word in the hustle of our lives. Sometimes we just don't know what or how to go about this devotional time, and so we skip it. We think we can keep going. We think we can do it on our own if we just stay organized enough.

The third lie addresses a conflict between our culture and God's Word. This lie is about the value of being a wife and mother. For the last few decades, our society has been trying to tell women that they can't possibly be fulfilled by staying at home and raising their children. They must be out in the workforce in order to be truly happy and to reach their fullest potential. Women need to understand that caring for their homes and families is central to their calling and is indeed a fulfilling job that reaps rich rewards.

Exploring the Truth . . .

Day One

God's Priorities, pp. 115–21

Realize

1. Where do you generally fall on each of the following scales, as it relates to your priorities, your schedule, and your use of time?

Peaceful, calm	1	2	3	4	5	Stressed, frazzled
Well ordered	1	2	3	4	5	Out of control
Purposeful use of time	1	2	3	4	5	Reacting to life
Good steward of time	1	2	3	4	5	Waste a lot of time
Balanced priorities	1	2	3	4	5	Overwhelmed by demands
Fulfilling His "to do" list for me	1	2	3	4	5	Frustrated by unfinished tasks
Relaxed spirit	1	2	3	4	5	Uptight spirit
Putting "first things first"	1	2	3	4	5	"Majoring on the minors"
Led by the Spirit	1	2	3	4	5	Driven by others or circumstances

Reflect

2. The word "priority" comes from the Latin word *prior*, which means "first." Our priorities are the things that take "first place" in our time and attention. We all live by priorities. The question is: are we living by the right priorities? Are we putting the first things first? Read Matthew 6:25–34 and Luke 10:38–42. What are some of the things that compete for "first place" in our lives? What should be the top priorities for every child of God?

_____

_____

3. Read Proverbs 3:5–6. What are some of the consequences we might experience if we rely on our own understanding rather than looking to God to direct our schedule and order our priorities?

_____

_____

4. According to the verses you just read and Proverbs 2:1–6, how can we discern what responsibilities God is assigning us and what is merely on our own "to do" list?

_____

_____

Respond

5. Complete this sentence: From now on, before I take on any more activities, I will seek God's guidance first by . . .

_____

_____

6. Write out a brief prayer of commitment, expressing your desire to know and to do the will of God and to have His priorities in your life.

_____

_____

Lord, I want to live according to Your priorities for my life. Please lead me and give me wisdom; teach me what things really matter to You. Help me to make the necessary adjustments in my schedule so that I might use the days You have given me to fulfill Your agenda. Amen.

Day Two

Jesus' Example, pp. 117–21

Realize

1. Near the end of His earthly ministry, Jesus said to His Father, "I have glorified You on the earth. I have finished the work which You have given Me to do" (John 17:4 NKJV). What does this verse reveal about Jesus' goals and priorities for His life?

_____

_____

2. According to Acts 20:24, how were the apostle Paul's goals and priorities similar to those of the Lord Jesus?

_____

_____

Reflect

3. If your goal in life is to glorify God and to finish the work He has given you to do, how should that affect your daily schedule and the way you use your time?

_____

_____

4. What helpful insight does Ephesians 2:10 give regarding the specific responsibilities and activities of believers? What difference can this perspective make as you seek to live a well-ordered, godly life?

_____

_____

Respond

5. Describe your typical day (or week). List the activities in which you are involved on a regular basis.

_____

_____

_____

6. Consider the activities above that are "negotiable." Does each of these activities fit in with your (and God's) priorities? Why or why not?

_____

_____

7. Prioritize each of the negotiable activities by ranking them with numbers. Are you tending to the top priorities? If not, what can you do now in order to simplify your schedule and your life so that you are acting on what is most important? Ask God what adjustments He wants you to make in your schedule, so that you can be sure you are glorifying Him and fulfilling His agenda for your life.

_____

_____

8. What do you need to do in order to be able to go to bed each night and say, "Today I finished the work that the Lord gave me to do"?

_____

_____

Lord, You know my schedule and all the demands that seem to come at me from every direction. Please help me make wise choices regarding my daily activities, so that at the end of the day I can say that I finished the work that You gave me to do. Amen.

Day Three

Time in the Word, pp. 121–4

Realize

1. According to the following verses in Psalm 119, what are some of the characteristics and functions of the Word of God?

- v. 9

  _____

  _____

- vv. 25, 28

  _____

  _____

- vv. 50, 52

  _____

  _____

- v. 72

  _____

  _____

- vv. 98–100

  _____

  _____

- vv. 104–105, 130

  _____

  _____

- v. 165

  _____

  _____

Reflect

2. Read Job 23:12 and Matthew 4:4. What do these verses help us understand about the priority of consistent intake of the Word of God into our lives? In what sense is "feeding" on the Word even more important than eating physical food?

  _____

  _____

3. Describe your current season of life. (In other words, you're chasing tod-dlers all day, you're working, you're running kids to and from activities, you're an empty nester.) Considering your current season, list below sev-eral specific areas in your life where you need God's help, guidance, wis-dom, or comfort.

_____

_____

4. As you look over your list, what are some ways the Word of God could meet your current needs?

_____

_____

Respond

5. What phrase best describes your spiritual condition, based on your intake of God's Word over the past six months?

_____ seriously malnourished—almost no nourishment

_____ poor diet—barely subsisting on minimum levels

_____ healthy—consistent, balanced diet

6. What practical action can you take to increase your daily intake of the Word of God and make your time alone with Him a greater priority?

_____

_____

Lord, I realize my need to spend time in Your Word every day. Please give me
a greater hunger to read and meditate on Your Word. Speak to me through
its pages. Change my life as I encounter You in Your Word. Amen.

Day Four

Time in Prayer, pp. 121–4

Realize

1. Read Matthew 14:23; Mark 1:35; and Luke 6:12; 9:28. Jesus had a habit of going off alone to pray. Why do you think prayer was such a priority for Jesus?

_____

_____

2. Read 1 Samuel 23:2, 4 and Psalm 5:3. How is David's life an example of the importance of prayer?

_____

_____

Reflect

3. Do you have a daily habit of spending time alone with God, reading His Word and praying? If not, what usually gets in the way?

_____

_____

4. Think about a day when you tried to "run on your own steam." How did things go? In what ways is your life different when you spend time alone talking with God?

_____

_____

Respond

5. How can you follow Jesus' example regarding time alone with God? (And that doesn't necessarily mean that you have to get up every day while it's still dark—although that might work for you!)

_____

_____

6. If you are struggling with having a regular quiet time because of a busy schedule, then schedule it. Ask the Lord to lead you as to when is the best time for you. Write down a specific time each day that you will set aside for an appointment with God.

_____

Note from Nancy

"Sometimes I get the sense that God may be saying to me, 'You want to handle this day by yourself? Go ahead.' The result? At best, an empty, fruitless day lived by and for myself. At worst, oh, what a mess I end up making of things. . . . When I start the day by humbling myself and acknowledging that I can't make it on my own—that I need Him—I can count on His divine enabling to carry me through the day" (p. 123).

Father, I want to cultivate a more intimate relationship with You.
Please teach me to pray. Give me the desire and the discipline to
spend time each day communicating with You. Amen.

Day Five

The Heart of Your Home, pp. 124–31

Realize

1. Read and meditate on Proverbs 31:10–31. These verses are not requiring you to be superwoman; instead, they present a portrait of a woman whose life is ordered around God-honoring priorities. What do you learn from her about the priorities of a woman who "fears the Lord"?

_____

_____

Note from Nancy

"The Scripture is clear that a married woman's life and ministry are to be centered in her home. This is not to suggest that it is necessarily wrong for a wife and mother to have a job outside her home—unless that job in any way competes with or diminishes her effectiveness in fulfilling her primary calling at home. Further, it is important for women to evaluate their reason(s) for working outside their home and to identify any deception behind those reasons" (pp. 127–8).

Reflect

2. What are some of the consequences our culture has reaped as a result of women's hearts being lured away from their homes?

_____

_____

3. Why is the family so important in God's economy? Why are the roles of "wife" and "mother" so vital in building strong homes?

_____

_____

4. What are some practical ways women can demonstrate the priority they place on their roles as wives and mothers?

_____

_____

Respond

5. *For wives and moms:* Ask God to show you if there are any secondary priorities that have infringed on your primary calling as a wife and mother. Record anything He places on your heart. What changes do you need to make in order to be faithful in fulfilling your responsibility to your family?

_____

_____

6. *For single women without children:* As a part of the body of Christ, how can you encourage other women in their callings as wives and mothers? What are some practical ways you can invest your time and energies in the family of God?

_____

_____

Thank You, Lord, for the distinctive calling You have given to women in their homes.
I want to fulfill the role for which You created me. If there are changes I need to make
in my priorities, please show me what I need to do and give me the courage to do it.
Help me to make our home a safe harbor for my family. Come into our home and
make it a place where You are known and loved and revealed. Amen.

Walking Together in the Truth . . .

1. In your reading and study of chapter 5, what truth did you find especially encouraging or helpful? (See page 132 in *Lies Women Believe*.) Did you find any of these truths difficult to accept?

   _____

   _____

Lie: I don't have time to do everything I'm supposed to do.

Truth: There is time in every twenty-four-hour day to do everything that is on God's "to do" list for my life.

2. How can knowing and believing this truth liberate us from false expectations?

   _____

   _____

3. What are some of the reasons that many women take on more responsibilities than God intends for them to have? What are the results of trying to do things that are not God's priority for this season of our lives?

   _____

   _____

4. Why is it important to consider the particular season of life that we are in as we evaluate and modify our priorities?

   _____

   _____

5. As opportunities arise for activities to be added to your schedule, how can you decide what is God's priority for you?

   _____

   _____

Note from Nancy

"I find that women (and Christian women are no exception) feel overwhelmed by how much they have to do and how little time they have to do it. As a result, many women are living breathless, frazzled, discouraged lives" (p. 117).

6. What role can other believers (husband, parents, godly friends, older women) play in helping us maintain God's priorities for our lives and daily schedules? How can we take advantage of this resource?

_____

_____

Lie: I can make it without consistent time in the Word and prayer.

Truth: It is impossible for me to be the woman God wants me to be apart from spending consistent time cultivating a relationship with Him in the Word and prayer.

7. Why do you think we often find it so difficult to make reading the Bible and prayer a priority in our lives?

_____

_____

8. Share your answer to question 5 on page 46. Share any specific commitment the Lord led you to make this week regarding your personal devotional life. (This is a great opportunity to encourage each other by offering prayer and accountability through the weeks ahead.)

_____

_____

Note from Nancy

"In determining our priorities as Christian women, we must first ask: Why did God make women? What is His purpose and mission for our lives? The Word of God provides women of every generation and culture with the Truth about our created purpose and primary role and calling. When we embrace the Truth and establish our priorities and schedules around it, we experience true liberation" (p. 126).

Lie: A career outside the home is more valuable and fulfilling than being a wife and mother.

Truth: In the will of God, there is no higher calling for a woman than being a wife and mother, serving her family, and devoting her attention and efforts to ministering to the needs of her husband and children.

9. In what ways does our culture downgrade the "career" of being a wife and mother?

_____

_____

10. Read 1 Timothy 5:9–10 and Titus 2:4–5. What do these passages tell us about God's priorities for Christian women?

_____

_____

11. Share with each other any convictions God has been putting on your heart about the need to focus more on ministering to the needs of your family.

CHAPTER

6

Honoring God in My Marriage

In a Nutshell . . .

This chapter and the next deal with the practical areas of marriage and family. If you are unmarried or do not have children, you may be tempted to skip over these chapters. However, it is important for every believer, in any season of life, to understand the Truth about these topics.

Nowhere is it more challenging to walk in the Truth than inside the four walls of our own homes. And nowhere have most of us experienced greater consequences of deception—hurt, failure, and confusion—than in the area of family relationships. Several of the topics that are addressed in these chapters are "hot potatoes"—issues where the teaching of God's Word flies in the face of what is politically correct. The intent of this study is not to stir up controversy but to challenge women to evaluate every area of their lives in light of the Scripture.

If you find yourself struggling with some of the concepts in these chapters, ask the Lord to help you honestly consider whether the things you believe are based on His Word or on your feelings or the input of others. The important issue is not that you agree with everything in this book but that you study God's Word and submit yourself to its authority.

Chapter 6 deals with the topic of marriage. Both married women and unmarried women struggle with the first lie in this chapter, which equates having a husband to being happy in life. Often, single women think that they must get married before they can be happy, and married women think that their husbands' purpose in life is to make them happy. Both are lies. Many women look to men to meet their needs rather than looking to God. People are imperfect and will disappoint us. Only God will never disappoint us.

The second lie begins to emerge after a woman marries and realizes that her knight in shining armor has a few chinks and rusty spots. She then sets about to change him, fix him, and make him a better person. Even if she truly desires to help him, that approach is likely to drive him away—relationally if not physically. A loving wife needs to use her "weapons" of godly living and prayer in order to truly help her husband become the man God wants him to be. Even if her husband never changes, she will be able to live at peace.

The third lie suggests that a woman has a right to expect her husband to serve her. Of course, a loving husband will want to serve his wife. But if she focuses on how he should help her, rather than on how she can be his "helper," she will experience disappointment and frustration.

The fourth lie is a multifaceted and prevalent one in our culture, for it introduces the "s" word—submission. Our society has pummeled this word to death, and even some within the church have attempted to sidestep it. However, biblical submission of the wife to her husband is simply the framework that makes a marriage operate in a healthy manner. When women are willing to let their husband lead, they are practicing biblical submission and demonstrating trust in God's authority over their husband.

The fifth lie is especially pervasive in an era characterized by passive men and aggressive women. Frustrated by husbands who won't lead, many women assume that role by default. The problem is that their doing so tends to exacerbate the problem instead of solving it.

Finally, the sixth lie has become so ingrained in our society that divorce has become almost "normal," and people who stay married are considered "abnormal." With few exceptions, most people today believe that it is better to divorce than to stay in a "bad marriage." The Scripture points us to the Truth about God's purposes and design for marriage, which can enable us to patiently work through difficulties rather than running from them through divorce, no matter how desirable that option may seem.

Exploring the Truth . . .

Day One

Expectations of Marriage, pp. 135–40

Note: If you are not currently married, feel free to skip over any questions in this week's study that do not apply directly to you.

Realize

1. How does our culture promote unrealistic expectations of marriage?

   _____

   _____

2. What is an expectation you had prior to marriage that you found to be unrealistic after getting married?

   _____

   _____

Reflect

3. Read Psalm 62:5, 118:8–9, and Jeremiah 17:5–8. Why is it foolish to look to people to satisfy us and meet our needs? Where should we focus our expectations?

_____

_____

4. Reflect on your marriage or, if you aren't married, on your desire for a husband. Are you expecting a man to meet needs in your life that only God can meet? What are those needs?

_____

_____

Note from Nancy

"Women who get married for the purpose of finding happiness are setting themselves up for almost certain disappointment; they seldom find what they are looking for" (pp. 137–8).

Respond

5. Have you made your husband a prisoner of your expectations by putting pressure on him to satisfy you and make you happy? Ask God to help you release your husband, and choose to place your hope wholly in God.

_____

_____

6. What is the ultimate source of true happiness? What biblical counsel would you give to a woman who says her husband is not making her happy? To a single woman who is finding it difficult to be content without a husband?

_____

_____

Lord, I thank You for my situation in life. I pray that You will help me not to look to other people to meet my needs but to look only to You. I realize that no human being can control my happiness; ultimately, I may choose to live in joy because of my relationship with You. Amen.

Day Two
Letting Go, pp. 140–2

Realize

1. While our intentions in wanting to change our husbands may be good in our own eyes, what does the Bible say about women who constantly harp on their husbands? (Read Proverbs 17:1; 19:13; 21:9.)

_____

_____

Note from Nancy

"Many Christian wives do not realize that they have two powerful 'weapons' available to them. . . . The first weapon is a godly life. . . . The second weapon is prayer. When a wife consistently points out the things she wishes her husband would change, she is likely to make him defensive and resistant. But when she takes her concerns to the Lord, she is appealing to a higher power to act in her husband's life . . . " (p. 141).

Reflect

2. Do you feel frustrated by things in your husband's life that you wish would change? If so, how have you been handling those feelings (e.g., ignoring them, ignoring him, nagging, telling your friends, worrying, etc.)?

_____

_____

3. What perspective and hope does Proverbs 21:1 offer about these things that need to be changed in your husband's life?

_____

_____

4. In what ways could living a godly life before your husband be beneficial for both him and you?

_____

_____

5. In what ways can you pray for your husband so that you are truly turning your burden over to the Lord? What if you don't see any answers for years?

_____

_____

Respond

6. Read Matthew 7:1–5. Would you want God and others to deal with your imperfections in the same way you deal with your husband's flaws?

_____

_____

7. What "plank" may you have missed in your own eye, while you have been so focused on trying to get rid of the "speck" in your husband's eye? Ask God to help you see the things in your life that need to be changed.

_____

_____

Lord, I understand that I need to let You work in my life and in my husband's life.
Help me not to be nagging, accusatory, or angry. Teach me how to live an upright life
before my husband and to bring the burdens I feel about him to You in prayer. Lord,
help me to wait on You and trust You to fulfill Your purposes in both our lives. Amen.

Day Three

A Virtuous Woman, pp. 142–5

Realize

1. Read Matthew 20:28; John 13:1–5, 12–17; and Philippians 2:5–7. What does it mean to be a servant? How did Jesus demonstrate the heart of a servant? What do we learn from His example about our calling as His followers?

_____

_____

Note from Nancy

"We are never more like Jesus than when we are serving Him or others. There is no higher calling than to be a servant" (p. 144).

Reflect

2. According to Genesis 2:18, God made the woman to be a "helper suitable" to her husband. What are some practical ways a wife might fulfill that role?

_____

_____

3. The virtuous woman in Proverbs 31:10–31 is probably a composite of the virtuous qualities in many women. What can you learn from her about serving your husband and family?

_____

_____

4. How can a woman develop and maintain a servant's heart when she feels that she is being taken advantage of or that no one appreciates what she does?

_____

_____

Respond

5. What are five practical ways you can demonstrate the servant heart of Jesus toward your husband this week?

_____

_____

_____

6. List some ways that your husband serves you. How will you thank him for those acts of service?

_____

_____

Lord Jesus, You came to this earth to be a servant. I want to be like You.

Yet serving is difficult sometimes: it can be such a thankless and lonely job.

Help me to serve my husband and family as if I were serving You. Amen.

Day Four

The Power of Submission, pp. 146–56

Realize

1. Read Ephesians 5:22–33. In what ways should a Christian marriage be a picture of the redemptive relationship between Christ and His church?

_____

_____

2. According to verses 22 and 33, what are the two ways wives are called to respond to their husbands?

_____

_____

Note from Nancy

"Satan has done a masterful job of convincing women that submission is a narrow, negative, and confining concept. . . . [He] knows that if we could see the Truth about biblical submission—one of the most liberating principles in all of God's Word—we would joyfully embrace it" (p. 146).

Reflect

3. How does submission to God-ordained authority reveal that we are trusting in God?

_____

_____

4. What happens when a woman becomes frustrated with her husband's leadership (or lack of leadership) and takes matters into her own hands? How does that affect her, her husband, and their relationship?

_____

_____

Respond

5. *Married women:* What is one specific area where you need to pray and wait on the Lord to change your husband's heart, rather than jumping in to handle the matter yourself?

_____

_____

Unmarried women: Even apart from marriage, women can affirm appropriate male leadership by making room for men to take initiative. What is one way you can do this in your relationship with a man such as your father, your employer, or your pastor?

_____

_____

6. *Married women:* How do your responses and your attitude toward your husband measure up to the standard of Ephesians 5?

_____

_____

Unmarried women: How well are you submitting to whatever human authorities God has placed over you?

_____

_____

Lord, I confess that I often struggle against submission. Help me to show my submission to You by the way I respond to my husband's leadership. Thank You that even when my husband (or another authority) fails, I can trust You to protect me as I walk in submission to Your Word. Amen.

Day Five

The Covenant of Marriage, pp. 156–61

Realize

1. Read and summarize what the Bible says about marriage in Genesis 2:18–24; Malachi 2:13–16; and Mark 10:2–12. Why is marriage a lifetime, binding relationship? How does divorce mar God's design?

_____

_____

2. What does Ecclesiastes 5:4–6 tell us about God's perspective on vows? What are the consequences of breaking a vow? (Note: If physical danger or abuse is involved, a woman should seek protection, direction, and intervention from the appropriate civil and/or spiritual authorities, rather than attempting to handle the situation on her own.)

_____

_____

Note from Nancy

"The primary purpose of marriage is not to be happy, but to glorify God and reflect His redeeming, covenant love. . . . No sooner does a couple say, 'I do,' than the Serpent rears his ugly head and sets out to destroy that marriage. He knows every divorce is an attack on the character of God and on the earthly picture of divine redemption" (pp. 156, 159).

Reflect

3. Read Psalm 89:33–34 and Isaiah 54:10. What do these verses tell us about the character of God? What are the implications for our lives, as we seek to be like Him and reflect His image in our marriages?

_____

_____

4. Review the list of truths about marriage on pages 159–60 of *Lies Women Believe*. In your own words, write out any that apply to a challenge you may be facing in your marriage or that you could share with a friend who is in a difficult marriage.

_____

_____

_____

Respond

5. In prayer, claim these truths, and ask God to help you to be faithful to Him and to your mate, no matter how difficult it may feel. In your own words, express below your commitment to be faithful to your marriage vows and to reflect the covenant-keeping heart of God.

_____

_____

Note: If you are divorced, remember that the grace of God can turn "ashes to beauty." He loves you and wants the very best for you. If your husband violated his vow toward you, what steps can you take toward completely forgiving him and finding healing and wholeness in Christ? If you were responsible for breaking your marriage vow, what steps do you need to take to be right with God and with your husband?

Thank You, Lord, for being faithful, even when we are unfaithful to You. I recognize that we need Your presence and power if our marriage is going to reflect You and bring You glory. Please give me grace to be faithful to You and faithful to my husband. In the difficult times, help me to walk in humility, love, and forgiveness, and to trust You to work in our lives and our marriage. Amen.

Walking Together in the Truth . . .

1. In your reading and study of chapter 6, what truth did you find especially encouraging or helpful? (See pages 162–3 in *Lies Women Believe*.) Did you find any of these truths difficult to accept?

_____

_____

Lie: I have to have a husband to be happy.

Truth: Happiness is not found in (or out of) marriage. No one person can meet my needs or make me truly happy. True joy can only be found through Christ.

2. Why is it dangerous for a woman to think she must have a husband in order to be happy and then to rely on her husband to make her happy? How does having unrealistic expectations for marriage set women up for disappointment?

_____

_____

3. How can women who are in difficult marriages find true joy and bring glory to God?

_____

_____

Lie: It is my responsibility to change my mate.

Truth: A godly life and prayer are a wife's two greatest means of influencing her husband.

4. What problems arise when a wife continually focuses on her husband's faults or tries to take God's responsibility for changing her husband?

_____

_____

5. Read James 5:16 and 1 Peter 3:1. How can we effectively use our tools of godly living and prayer in dealing with our husbands? How will these help them and us?

_____

_____

Note from Nancy

"If we as women focus on what we 'deserve,' on our 'rights,' or on what men 'ought' to do for us, we will become vulnerable to hurt and resentment when our expectations are not fulfilled. Blessing and joy are the fruit of seeking to be a giver rather than a taker . . ." (p. 143).

"If we as women focus on what we 'deserve,' on our 'rights,' or on what men 'ought' to do for us, we will become vulnerable to hurt and resentment when our expectations are not fulfilled. Blessing and joy are the fruit of seeking to be a giver rather than a taker . . ." (p. 143).

Lie: My husband is supposed to serve me.

Truth: If I expect to be served, I will be disappointed. If I seek to serve without expecting anything in return, I will never be disappointed.

6. Share an illustration of this quote from Nancy—either an experience out of your own life or one that you have observed in someone else's.

   _____

   _____

Lie: If I submit to my husband, I'll be miserable!

Truth: Submission places me under the covering and protection of God.

7. What benefits does a wife experience when she lives in submission to God and to her husband?

   _____

   _____

8. What are some possible consequences of a wife's resisting God-ordained authority or failing to reverence her husband?

   _____

   _____

9. Share one blessing (or consequence) you have experienced as a result of submitting (or not submitting) to the authority of your husband (or, if you are unmarried, to another authority).

   _____

   _____

10. In what ways can women emasculate their husbands by taking the role that their husbands are supposed to have? What effect could that have in a marriage?

   _____

Lie: If my husband is passive, I've got to take the initiative, or nothing will get done.

Truth: In God's design for marriage, the husband is the initiator. If a woman takes the reigns rather than waiting on God to move her husband, her husband is likely to be less motivated to fulfill his God-given responsibility.

11. When a woman determines to wait on the Lord rather than taking the reigns, what blessings could result in her life? In her husband? In her marriage?

_____

_____

Note from Nancy

"A wife's submission to her husband, regardless of his spiritual condition, actually releases her from fear because she has entrusted herself to God, who has ultimate control of her husband and her situation" (p. 150).

Lie: Sometimes divorce is a better option than staying in a bad marriage.

Truth: Marriage is a lifelong covenant. There is no marriage that God cannot heal. There is no person God cannot change. God's grace is sufficient, even in the most difficult or extreme circumstances.

12. Take time to pray together for the marriages represented in your group. (If your group is too large or you are under time constraints, you may want to pray in smaller groups or exchange names to pray for each other during the week ahead.)

• Pray that each marriage would bring glory to God and would become a picture of His redeeming love.

• Pray that each partner would commit to the permanence of marriage and would accept and live out God's role for him or her in the marriage.

• Pray for spiritual protection from every form of deception and from the schemes of Satan.

• Pray for those marriages that are struggling. Ask God to grant humility and grace to work through any issues that are causing conflict.

Raising Children

In a Nutshell . . .

Good blessed women with the unique ability to bear and nurture children. If you ask almost any mother what is most important in her life, she will tell you, "My children." Chapter 7 deals with several subtle lies and half-truths about children and parenting that have become widely accepted in our culture. Many Christian women have simply adopted the world's way of thinking without stopping to evaluate how those beliefs line up with God's Word.

As with some other controversial topics in this book, the positions taken in this chapter are not the final word. They simply reflect my understanding of what the Scripture teaches. My primary concern is not that you agree with me but that you make the effort to examine the Word for yourself to make sure that your beliefs and practices are rooted in Truth.

The first area where many women have been deceived is in the matter of childbearing. The world promotes the idea that children are a burden and that every woman has the right to determine if and when she will have children. God's Word teaches, on the other hand, that children are a blessing, a gift from God, and a vital part of His plan for passing the Truth on to the next generation. As we trust God in other areas of our lives, so we can trust Him in relation to the timing and size of our families.

The second lie affects many practical decisions parents make for their children. Many parents believe that their children need to be exposed to the "real world" so they can learn to function in it. The truth is that God never intended for us to know evil by experiencing it for ourselves. It is important that children be sheltered and protected from personal exposure to evil until they have had time to develop a love for God and a good understanding of right and wrong. Then, when they are exposed to the culture, they will be able to make good choices based on firm convictions.

The third lie is the assumption that all children must go through a rebellious stage. The truth is that if parents expect their children to rebel, then they probably will. God's Word exhorts Christian parents to lead their children to follow the Lord. The Bible offers hope that, by God's grace, the faith of godly parents really can be passed on intact to their children.

The fourth lie is a subtle one. Some parents assume that their children are believers because they prayed to receive Christ at a young age, even though, years later, their children's lives do not demonstrate evidence of genuine conversion. Such parents may be giving their children a false sense of security and may need to refocus their prayers for their children.

The fifth lie promotes two extremes: The first is that parents are not responsible at all for how their children turn out; the second is that parents are 100 percent responsible. Neither is true. Parents are responsible to raise their children according to the principles of God's Word, with the understanding that their children must make personal commitments to Christ and that they are ultimately responsible for their own choices.

Exploring the Truth . . .

Day One

The Blessing of Children, pp. 167–72

Note: Again in this chapter, simply skip any questions that do not apply to you if you are not a mom.

Realize

1. Read the following verses: Psalm 113:9; 127:3–5; and Matthew 19:13–15. What do they tell us about God's view of children?

   _____

   _____

2. How is the world's view of children different than God's view?

   _____

   _____

Reflect

3. This issue is probably the most controversial one addressed in *Lies Women Believe*. Why do you think this subject evokes such a strong reaction from so many women?

   _____

   _____

4. What are some of the factors that commonly influence people's decisions about the size and timing of their family? Put a check mark next to any factors that have influenced your decisions in this area.

_____

_____

Note from Nancy

"The process by which most people—even 'believers'—determine the size of their family is often driven by fear, selfishness, and natural, human reason" (p. 170).

5. The Scripture does not explicitly address the subject of birth control (except for the instance when Pharaoh forbade Jewish women from having children). However, it has much to say about children and childbearing: for example,

   • children are a blessing and a gift from God;

   • they are a primary means of passing the faith from one generation to the next;

   • God is the One who opens and shuts the womb; childbearing is a primary purpose of marriage (Malachi 2:15);

   • the willingness to bear children is a vital evidence of a woman's faith (1 Timothy 2:15; 5:14).

   We also know that God is sovereign and that He can be trusted (Jeremiah 29:11). What implications would these truths have for a couple as they make decisions related to childbearing?

   _____

   _____

Respond

6 Would you say that your decisions in relation to childbearing have been based on . . .

   • fear or faith?

   _____

   • natural, human reasoning or biblical thinking?

   _____

   • selfish motives or a commitment to the kingdom of God?

   _____

   • personal emotions and desires or a sincere desire to honor God?

   _____

7. If you have any doubt or confusion as to whether your position on childbearing is pleasing to the Lord, write out a prayer asking God to show you the Truth and to give you the faith and courage to walk in the Truth.

   _____

   _____

8. Sometimes it's easy to forget that your children really are a blessing! If you have children, write their names and ages below. Next to each name write a phrase or two explaining how that child has been a blessing to you.

_____

_____

_____

*Lord, thank You for the gift of children. Help me to welcome them even
as You do. Show me how to fulfill my calling as a woman—to be a bearer
and nurturer of life, whether that means having physical children of my
own or "mothering" spiritual children You entrust to me. Amen.*

Day Two

Protecting Your Children, pp. 173–6

Realize

1. Children are a valuable treasure; they must be carefully protected, cared for, and nurtured. As you would protect a delicate seedling from winter storms and regularly give it water, what are some things you can do to care for your precious "seedlings"—your children?

   • Protect them

   _____

   _____

   • Give them

   _____

   _____

2. Read Psalm 101. In your own words, summarize what these verses say about the environment parents should seek to create in their homes.

   _____

   _____

3. Read Psalm 92:13–15. What encouragement do these verses give to parents who seek to raise their children in a Christ-centered environment?

   _____

   _____

Reflect

4. While God does not intend us to know evil by experiencing it ourselves, our children need to understand that evil exists and to learn to discern between good and evil. How can parents help their children develop that kind of discernment without exposing them to influences from which they should be protected?

_____

_____

5. Read Matthew 5:13–16. What are some practical ways you can give your children a vision for becoming a righteous influence in an unrighteous world?

_____

_____

_____

Respond

6. If you have children still living at home, prayerfully consider the various influences in their lives. Ask the Lord to show you any negative influences from which they need to be protected and any positive influences that need to be added. Write down any specifics He brings to mind.

• Entertainment (TV, movies, computer games, Internet)

_____

_____

• Reading (books, magazines)

_____

_____

• Music

_____

_____

• Friends

_____

_____

• Education (school, teachers, textbooks)

_____

_____

Note from Nancy

"God never intended that you and I should know evil by experiencing it ourselves. . . . The Truth is, our task is not to rear children who can 'fit in' or merely 'survive' in this world. The challenge of every Christian parent is to bring up children who love God with all their hearts, souls, minds, and strength . . . children who enthusiastically embrace the Truth . . . who love righteousness and hate evil . . . who will be used by God to change this world" (p. 173).

- Atmosphere and example in the home

_____

_____

Lord, please make me discerning and alert to protect my children from
evil influences, even if that means being different than others around us.
Give my children a desire for what is holy, true, and good. Help me to model
right choices for them. I pray that my children will grow up to love You
with all their hearts and to bring You glory in this world. Amen.

Day Three

Avoiding Rebellion, pp. 176–9

Realize

1. Read Psalm 78:1–7. Describe the responsibility God gives parents for their children and grandchildren. What outcome does the psalmist encourage parents to anticipate as a result of their obedience? What resources does God make available to fulfill this responsibility?

_____

_____

Note from Nancy

"Christian parents have been given a sacred mandate to lead their children to submit their lives to Jesus as Lord and to take their children with them into the 'ark of salvation.' That high and holy calling is accompanied by the divine resources of His Spirit and His promises" (p. 177).

2. Read Genesis 18:17–19. What vision did God give Abraham for his role as a father and for his children and the generations to follow?

_____

_____

Reflect

3. God has not left parents without the necessary resources to fulfill their calling with their children. He gives parents His Spirit, His Word, faith, prayer, humility, discipline, instruction, the power of godly modeling, love, the grace of God, and the body of Christ. Select two or three of these resources that you need to take greater advantage of in your home. Explain how each could assist you in leading your children to follow Christ?

_____

_____

_____

4. The promises of God are another resource for parents. Read Psalm 103:17–18 and Acts 2:39. How do these verses give hope to parents who walk with God?

_____

_____

Respond

5. If you have a child who is rebelling, how can you best help him through this difficult time so that he has the least amount of regrets or lifelong consequences?

_____

_____

6. In what ways can you give each of your children a vision of the purpose and plans God has for his or her life?

_____

_____

_____

Father, I cry out to You on behalf of my children and plead with You for wisdom to know how to lead them. Help me to communicate Your ways to them, and show me how to rely on Your resources. I pray that you will open their hearts to the Truth, that their wills will be brought into submission to Yours, and that You will protect them from choices they will one day regret. Amen.

Day Four

Your Children's Faith, pp. 179–82

Realize

1. According to the following verses, what are some of the evidences of genuine conversion?

• 2 Corinthians 5:17

_____

• Hebrews 3:14

_____

• 1 John 2:3–5

_____

Note from Nancy

"The Scripture is clear that a person may know all about God, say all the right things, and even have deeply religious experiences—without ever being converted" (p. 180).

- 1 John 3:14–15

  _____

- 1 John 4:13, 15

  _____

Reflect

2. Before parents can pray wisely about the spiritual condition of their children, they must have assurance of their own salvation. Based on the Scriptures above, what evidence does your life give of genuine conversion?

   _____

   _____

   _____

3. The Bible makes it clear that those who call upon the Lord are saved—and that applies to small children as well (Luke 18:16; Romans 10:13). How can parents encourage their children to place their trust in Christ without pushing them into a "decision" apart from the true conviction of sin and the drawing of the Spirit?

   _____

   _____

4. If your children are strong in their faith, how should you pray for them? If your children have not become believers or are living in ways that contradict their profession of faith, how should you pray for them?

   _____

   _____

5. Why is it important for parents to give their children spiritual training right from the start? What does the Bible say about training up our children (Proverbs 22:6; Ephesians 6:4)?

   _____

   _____

Respond

6. If your child is living apart from Christ, why is it dangerous to turn a blind eye to his need for salvation, assuming that in time he will return? What do you think God wants you to do for your straying child today? What does He promise (John 6:39; 2 Peter 3:9)?

   _____

   _____

Father, I want all of my children to become Your true children. I pray that Your Spirit

will bring each of my children to a point of genuine conviction and conversion.

May the fruit of my conversion and theirs be evident in the way we live. Amen.

Day Five

Shaping Your Children, pp. 182–7

Realize

1. Read 1 Thessalonians 1:2–6 and 2:3–13. This description of the apostle Paul's ministry has some striking applications for parents who want to see their children become followers of Christ. Record several insights from this passage about the qualities and actions of good discipleship.

_____

_____

2. According to these verses, what were the results of Paul's ministry in the lives of his spiritual children?

_____

_____

Reflect

3. One study indicated that eight out of ten young people who grow up in the church leave the church after high school, never to return. Why do you think so many children grow up in Christian homes, schools, and churches without ever developing a real heart for God?

_____

_____

Note from Nancy

"Parents have enormous influence and are responsible to mold the hearts and lives of their children. As easy as it is to shift blame to peers, teachers, entertainment, church youth groups, or secular culture, the fact is, we are accountable for the spiritual condition of the flock God has given us to shepherd" (p. 186).

4. Re-read 1 Thessalonians 2:10. Paul recognized the impact of his example on these young believers. In what areas do you believe you have set a good example for your children? In what areas would you not want them to follow your example?

_____

_____

5. Read 1 Thessalonians 2:11–12. Why is it important to provide a balance of warm encouragement and firm admonition for those we lead? Which of these generally comes more easily for you with your children? Which do you need to provide more of?

_____

_____

Respond

6. What character and spiritual qualities do you want your children to have when they leave home? How can you be more intentional about developing those qualities in their lives?

_____

_____

7. If your children end up being a mirror reflection of you, what will they look like? What changes do you need to allow the Lord to make in your life so that you can say to your children, "Imitate me, just as I also imitate Christ" (1 Corinthians 11:1)? (If you are really courageous, ask your children to answer these questions about their mother!)

_____

_____

Lord, it is sobering to realize how much our children pick up from our lives,
our values, and our walk with You. Please do whatever is needed to make
me the mother that my children need. May my life create in them a desire to
know and follow You. Please work in their lives to draw them to You,
that our family may reflect Your light to others. Amen.

Walking Together in the Truth . . .

1. In your reading and study of chapter 7, what truth did you find especially encouraging or helpful? (See pages 188–9 in *Lies Women Believe.*) Did you find any of these truths difficult to accept?

_____

_____

Lie: It's up to us to determine the size of our family.

Truth: God is the Creator and Giver of life. Anything that hinders or discourages women from fulfilling their God-given calling to be bearers and nurturers of life furthers Satan's schemes and aids his efforts.

2. Read Psalm 127:3–5. Why are children called a "reward"? In what ways has this proven true in your experience?

_____

_____

3. In what ways does the world sometimes discourage women from having children? How can Christian couples demonstrate the value that God places on children?

_____

_____

Note from Nancy

"Children will cultivate an appetite for whatever they are fed in their earliest, formative years" (p. 175).

4. What biblical counsel would you give to a woman who wants to have more children but whose husband thinks they have enough already?

_____

_____

Lie: Children need to get exposed to the "real world" so that they can learn to function in it.

Truth: Our task is not to raise children who can fit into this world or merely survive in it but to bring up children who will be used by God to change the world.

5. What kinds of influences in our culture do you think are particularly harmful to young children? How can Christian parents protect their children from unnecessary exposure to those influences?

_____

_____

6. I what ways can Christian parents help to cultivate in their children an appetite for God's Word, His Truth, and His ways?

_____

_____

Lie: All children will go through a rebellious stage.

Truth: Parents cannot force their children to walk with God, but they can model godliness and cultivate a climate in the home that creates an appetite for God and is conducive to the spiritual nurture and growth of their children.

Note from Nancy

"The essence of true salvation is not a matter of profession or performance; rather, it is a transformation. . . . The man or woman who has been truly converted has a new life, a new heart, a new nature, a new allegiance, and a new master" (p. 181).

7. What are some ways that parents can keep the lines of communication open during the changes and challenges of the teen years?

_____

_____

Note from Nancy

"The first [lie] is that [parents] have no control or influence over how their children have turned out—that they are not responsible, that the situation could not be helped. . . . The second lie parents believe is that they are 100 percent responsible for how their children have turned out—that it is all their fault" (p. 183).

Lie: I know my child is a Christian because he prayed to receive Christ at an early age.

Truth: Parents who assume their children know the Lord, regardless of their lifestyle, may be giving their children a false sense of security and may not be praying appropriately for their children.

8. How has our evangelical culture made it easier for people to profess faith in Christ without showing evidence of true conversion?

   _____

   _____

9. Why is it unwise and unloving to assume that a son or daughter is a believer, based solely on his or her profession of faith?

   _____

   _____

Lie: We are not responsible for how our children turn out.

Truth: Parents have enormous influence in molding the lives of their children by their example, their teaching, and their leadership.

10. Why are both of these extremes incorrect? What is the correct balance that parents must understand as they raise their children?

    _____

    _____

11. Read Deuteronomy 6:4–9 and Proverbs 4:11. What does the Scripture say about the importance of parents providing both a good example and solid instruction for their children?

    _____

    _____

12. Based on your study this week, what is one change the Lord is leading you to make or one step He is leading you to take as a parent?

    _____

    _____

13. Take time to pray (by name, if possible) for the children represented in your group.

    • Ask the Lord for wisdom and grace for each mother to know how to influence and mold her children's lives.

- Pray that the Holy Spirit will graciously intervene in each child's life, bringing him to true salvation and giving him a hunger for righteousness.

- Pray that each child will be protected from any harmful influences and will develop a love for righteousness and a hatred for evil.

- Pray that God's eternal purposes will be fulfilled in each child's life and that the baton of faith will be passed on intact to the next generation.

Note from Nancy

"Being a parent is a high and holy calling. There is no more demanding occupation. The best of parents are utterly dependent on the Holy Spirit to make it 'click' with their children. That is why a mother's greatest human resource is prayer" (p. 187).

Handling Emotions

In a Nutshell . . .

In chapter 8 we come to one of the most complex and difficult-to-understand aspects of our walk as women—our emotions. God created emotions; He experiences emotions and understands them. However, His emotions are always perfect, whereas ours have been tainted by sin. Our emotions can send us all kinds of mixed messages, often deceiving us and leading us away from the Truth. The best weapon against misleading emotions is to pinpoint the lies and learn to counteract them with the Truth.

The first lie tells us that when we feel something, it must be true. If we feel unloved, then we are. If we feel that God has deserted us, then He has. We need to counteract this lie with the truth that we cannot depend on our feelings to give us a true assessment of our situation. We should always rely on what we *know* to be true, regardless of how we *feel*.

The second lie gives control of our lives to our emotions, saying that we cannot control our emotions. We often use this belief to justify wrong actions or reactions on our part, rationalizing, "I can't help the way I feel." While it is true that we cannot necessarily control how we feel about something, we *can* control how much power we allow our feelings to have over our lives. We can always choose to obey God, regardless of how or what we are feeling.

The third lie sometimes gets us off the hook when we're just plain mean. Many women use their changing hormones as an excuse for abusive words, sinful actions, or generally shrewish behavior. "I can't help it," they say. "It's my hormones," or "It's that time of the month." The truth is that sinful behavior is never justified, regardless of what may be taking place in our bodies. As our Creator, God understands the hormonal changes associated with the changing cycles and seasons of our lives. His grace is available and sufficient to help us obey and glorify Him as we pass through every season of life.

The fourth lie has to do with how women deal with the increasingly common problem of depression. The widely accepted and promoted view today—even among Christians—is that the answer to depression must first be sought in medication or psychotherapy. The problem with that assumption is that in many cases, the physical and emotional symptoms of depression are the result of issues rooted within the soul or the spirit. If that is the case, medication or therapy may temporarily treat the symptoms, but they will not bring lasting change. Regardless of the cause of the depression, we must remember that God has not promised to provide relief from all our problems (here and now) or to make us feel good; He has promised to be with us and to give us grace to endure. Our goal should be to bring glory to God and to be sanctified through the pain.

Exploring the Truth . . .

Day One

Discerning Your Emotions, pp. 193–7

Realize

1. Read Deuteronomy 4:24; Psalm 30:5; 36:5; and Matthew 26:38. What are some of the emotions God experiences? Why is it important to understand that God expresses emotions?

   _____

   _____

2. Because we are made in God's image (Genesis 1:27), what does that mean about our emotions?

   _____

   _____

Reflect

3. Read Psalm 16:5–11. What words or phrases in this passage speak of positive emotional expressions? What causes such emotions to flow out of the psalmist's heart?

   _____

   _____

4. In what ways are our emotions tainted by the Fall? Describe how you have experienced that tainting of emotions in your life.

   _____

   _____

5. What are some of the things that can cause our feelings to fluctuate?

   _____

   _____

6. Why is it dangerous for us to live and act completely on the basis of our feelings?

_____

_____

7. Read Psalm 56:3–4. What is the role of faith in dealing with our emotions?

_____

_____

Respond

8. What is one feeling you have experienced recently that is not consistent with the Truth and needs to be rejected?

_____

_____

Note from Nancy

"The Truth is that, due to our fallen condition, our feelings often have very little to do with reality. In many instances, feelings are simply not a reliable gauge of what is actually true. . . . If we want to walk in freedom, we must realize that our emotions are not necessarily trustworthy and be willing to reject any feelings that are not consistent with the Truth" (p. 195).

Lord, I understand that my emotions are part of how You created me, yet many times they are unreliable because they are influenced by changing circumstances. Help me to reject any feelings that are not based on Truth and to trust Your Word rather than my feelings. Amen.

Day Two

Controlling Your Emotions, pp. 197–9

Realize

1. Describe a time when your emotions got the better of you—when you felt that your emotions were out of control.

_____

_____

2. How much do your emotions affect your actions on any given day?

_____

_____

Note from Nancy

"The Enemy uses this lie to make us believe we have no choice but to be controlled by our emotions. While it may be true to some degree that we can't help the way we feel, the Truth is that we don't have to let our feelings run our lives. . . . The Truth is . . . we can choose to fix our minds on Him . . ." (p. 197).

Reflect

3. Ephesians 4:26 says, "In your anger do not sin." The Bible acknowledges the reality of anger, but God expects us to control how we react when we are angry. The emotion of anger itself is not the sin but often prompts a sinful response. Which emotions do you have the hardest time controlling? What are some sinful ways you express those emotions?

   _____

   _____

4. Describe an occasion when you acted on your feelings in a sinful way.

   _____

   _____

5. Read Isaiah 26:3; Philippians 4:8–9; and Colossians 3:1–2. How can we be free from the control of feelings that are not based on Truth? Why is it so important to control what we think about?

   _____

   _____

6. What positive steps does the Scripture exhort us to take in dealing with runaway emotions?

   _____

   _____

Respond

7. What can you do today to fix your mind, thoughts, and heart on God and His Truth?

   _____

   _____

Father, sometimes my emotions do seem overwhelming. Thank You that I do not need to be controlled by my feelings. I pray that You will be Lord over every part of my life, including my emotions. Help me to set my thoughts and affections on You each moment of the day. Amen.

Day Three

Expressing Your Emotions, pp. 197–9

Realize

1. The Psalms are rich with the personal, emotional outpourings of the psalmists' hearts. What emotions are expressed in the following verses?

   Psalm 6:1–3

   _____

   _____

   Psalm 9:1–2

   _____

   _____

   Psalm 10:1

   _____

   _____

   Psalm 51:1–2

   _____

   _____

   Psalm 90:7–10

   _____

   _____

   Psalm 118:24

   _____

   _____

Reflect

2. Why is it significant that, in each of the passages above, the psalmist pours out his heart *to the Lord?*

   _____

   _____

3. Read Psalm 6. How did David bring God into his emotional struggle? How can expressing our feelings to God help us deal with runaway emotions?

   _____

   _____

4. What truths about God helped David find emotional stability in Psalm 6?

   _____

   _____

Note from Nancy

"The Scripture is filled with divine promises and commands that provide the means by which our emotions may be steadied in the midst of any storm" (p. 198).

5. Read 2 Peter 1:4. How can God's promises protect us from expressing our natural emotions in sinful ways?

   _____

   _____

6. Write down two biblical promises that you can turn to and rely on when you are feeling overwhelmed by negative emotions.

_____

_____

Respond

7. Review the list of promises and commands from God's Word on pages 198–9 of *Lies Women Believe*. Which promise or command can you claim or obey today to help steady any emotions you are feeling that may not be based on the Truth?

_____

_____

Thank You, Father, that I can pour out my heart to You when I am troubled.
Thank You for the many promises and commands in Your Word that can
protect me from sin. Help me to claim Your promises and look to You for
grace to obey Your commands, regardless of what I may be feeling. Amen.

Day Four

Facing Life's Changing Seasons, pp. 200–203

Realize

1. Describe what happens to you during "that time of the month." What physical and emotional changes do you experience?

_____

_____

2. How do you normally respond to those changes? Do your actions generally affect your relationships positively or negatively? Explain.

_____

_____

3. In what ways do you try to excuse your behavior—either aloud or just to yourself—when you don't feel well physically?

_____

_____

Reflect

4. Read Psalm 139:1–18 and Luke 12:7. How well does God know you? How is His intimate knowledge of you comforting?

_____

_____

5. List some divine resources that are available when your body is changing and you feel out of control (e.g., the grace of God).

_____

_____

Respond

6. What practical steps can you take to ensure that, even if you are experiencing physical changes and your emotions are swinging wildly, you do not act in a way that is displeasing to God or unloving toward others?

_____

_____

Note from Nancy

"Is it conceivable that this wise, loving Creator would be unaware of our hormone levels at any stage of maturity or would have failed to make provision for every season of life? He does not offer an easy or trouble-free process of growth. But He has promised to meet all our needs and to give us grace to respond to the challenges and difficulties associated with every stage of life" (p. 203).

Lord, I find it especially difficult to respond correctly to You and to others when certain changes are taking place in my body. I know that You created my body, that You control the changing cycles and seasons of life, and that You have the resources to help me through. Help me to honor You in each of those seasons. Amen.

Day Five

Dealing with Depression, pp. 204–10

Realize

1. Read Psalm 42. Describe some of the circumstances David was facing and how he was feeling when he wrote this psalm.

_____

_____

_____

2. Which verses in this passage show that David . . .

- was honest with God about how he was feeling?

  _____

- made himself face the root issues of his depression?

  _____

- turned to God in his depression?

  _____

- counseled his heart according to the Truth of God's character?

  _____

- exercised faith in God's ultimate victory over his feeling and circumstances?

  _____

Note from Nancy

"In many cases, physiological symptoms connected with depression are the fruit of issues that are rooted in the realm of the soul and spirit— issues such as ingratitude, unresolved conflict, irresponsibility, guilt, bitterness, unforgiveness, unbelief, claiming of rights, and self-centeredness" (pp. 204–5).

Reflect

3. It is commonly assumed today that depression is caused by physiological and neurological problems. But the Scriptures indicate that spiritual issues can actually produce physical and emotional symptoms of depression. Select two or three of those issues (see note to the left) and explain how they could contribute to symptoms of depression.

   _____

   _____

4. Describe an occasion when you experienced physical or emotional symptoms related to depression, as a result of one or more of these spiritual issues.

   _____

   _____

5. Select two or three of the following "divine resources" and explain why they are important in dealing with depression: prayer, forgiveness, confession of sin, obedience, acceptance, yielding "rights," the body of Christ, God's grace, the Word, praise, and faith.

   _____

   _____

   _____

6. Many Christians have experienced a "dark night of the soul," even while they are walking with God. Read Isaiah 50:10; Hebrews 4:14–16; and 12:3. According to God's Word, what should a believer do at such times?

   _____

   _____

Respond

7. Read Psalm 42:11. Write it in your own words below, putting your name where the psalmist says "O my soul." Write this verse on a card, and put it in a place where you will be reminded to quote it to yourself as needed.

_____

_____

Lord, You are my Light in the darkness, my Hope in times of despair, and my Helper
in life's most desperate hours. You lift up my head. No matter how great the darkness
I am experiencing emotionally, help me to look to You, to wait patiently for You, and
to trust that You are faithful and that Your mercy and grace will sustain me. Amen.

Walking Together in the Truth . . .

1. In your reading and study of chapter 8, what truth did you find especially encouraging or helpful? (See page 211 in *Lies Women Believe*.) Did you find any of these truths difficult to accept?

_____

_____

Lie: If I feel something, it must be true.

Truth: My feelings cannot always be trusted. They often have little to do with reality and easily deceive me. I must choose to reject any feelings that are not consistent with the Truth.

2. Describe a time when your emotions were misleading and didn't match what was really true in a situation. Did you choose to believe your feelings or did you reject your feelings and believe the Truth? What was the result?

_____

_____

Lie: I can't control my emotions.

Truth: I do not have to be controlled by my emotions. I can choose to fix my mind on the Truth, to take every thought captive to the Truth, and to let God control my emotions.

3. Read 2 Corinthians 10:5. How can you truly "take captive every thought to make it obedient to Christ"? What difference will that make in your life?

_____

_____

Note from Nancy

"Certainly what happens in our bodies does affect us emotionally, mentally, and even spiritually. We cannot isolate these various dimensions of who we are. . . . But we fall into the trap of the Enemy when we justify fleshly, sinful attitudes and responses based on our physical condition or hormonal changes" (p. 201).

Lie: I can't help how I respond when my hormones are out of whack.

Truth: By God's grace, I can choose to obey Him regardless of how I feel. There is no excuse for ungodly attitudes, responses, or behavior. My physical and emotional cycles and seasons are under the control of my Creator.

4. Hormonal changes are very real—no woman will contest that. What provision(s) has God made to help us deal with those changes in a way that glorifies Him?

_____

_____

5. In what ways can the fluctuating emotions that may accompany our monthly cycle (or pregnancy or menopause) actually draw us closer to the Lord?

_____

_____

Lie: The answer to depression must first be sought in medication and/or psychotherapy.

Truth: Physical and emotional symptoms of depression may be the fruit of issues in the spirit that need to be addressed. If depression did not originate as a physical problem, medication will not permanently relieve it.

6. Why do you think depression has become so widespread among women in the Western Hemisphere?

_____

_____

7. What are some of the heart issues that can cause physical or emotional symptoms of depression? Why is it important to deal with those issues?

_____

_____

8. What are some of the divine resources God has made available that can minister grace to a woman suffering from depression?

_____

_____

9. Read together Lamentations 3:1–33. Describe the anguish Jeremiah felt. In what did Jeremiah ultimately place his hope?

_____

_____

10. Encourage a few women in your group to share how they have experienced the truth of Lamentations 3:21–26 in their walk with God.

Note from Nancy

"We must remember that 'feeling good' is not the ultimate objective in the Christian's life. . . . As long as we are in these bodies, we will experience varying degrees of pain and distress. . . . The . . . focus of our lives must not be on changing or 'fixing' things to make ourselves feel better but on the glory of God and His redemptive purposes in the world. . . . True joy comes from abandoning ourselves to that end" (p. 210).

Dealing with Circumstances

In a Nutshell . . .

Chapter 9 applies to every one of us, for we all have "circumstances." Our situations in life are as varied as the people involved. How we react to our circumstances—whether we believe the lies presented to us or embrace God's Truth—has a profound effect on everything else. Some circumstances are beyond our control. If we fail to see the hand of God behind our circumstances, we will be vulnerable to confusion, frustration, bitterness, anger, and despair.

One lie many women believe is that if only their circumstances were different, then *they* would be different—they would act differently or they would be happier. What they are really saying is that they are victims of their circumstances, that they are powerless to control what they say or do. The truth is that we are not victims. Our circumstances do not *make* us what we are. They merely *reveal* what we are. We may not be able to control our circumstances; but by God's grace, we can choose how we respond to our circumstances.

Another way many believers have been deceived is by the idea that they shouldn't have to suffer. After all, as Christians, we should have lots of money, success, and no worries, right? Not necessarily. Jesus never promised an easy life. On the contrary, the Scriptures teach that it is impossible to become like Jesus—to be holy—apart from suffering. Because we don't understand the necessity and value of suffering, we are often more concerned about getting relief from our pain than about discovering the pure fruit God wants to produce in our lives through the pain.

Another lie we may fall for is that our circumstances will never change. If we believe this lie, we will grow discouraged and be tempted to give up when facing seemingly impossible circumstances. In order to walk in freedom, we must exchange our temporal, earthly perspective for a set of heavenly, eternal glasses. Even if nothing changes in our lifetime, the years we experience on this earth are a mere blip on the timeline of eternity. So, we can pray for God to intervene, but we must be patient when He does not act as quickly as we'd like. We must trust, obey, hope, and persevere even as we await His answers. And we must set our eyes on heaven!

The fourth lie deceives many people to give up and say they just can't take it anymore. They truly believe that God has placed too much in their lives. God promises, however, that His grace is sufficient to help us in our weakness.

Finally, the fifth lie seems to have found its way into the fabric of our selfish society—"It's all about me." Everything revolves around *me;* nothing is more important than *my* wants, *my* needs, *my* desires. This attitude has broken marriages, families, and hearts everywhere. The truth for believers is that this life is *not* all about them; it is all about God. He is the reason we exist, and we should live to honor and glorify Him.

Exploring the Truth . . .

Day One

Accepting Our Circumstances, pp. 215–21

Realize

1. Describe Eve's circumstances in the Garden, before the entrance of sin. In spite of an ideal setting, Eve managed to become discontent and make a wrong choice. What does that say about our circumstances and our choices?

_____

_____

Reflect

2. Look at the list of "if onlys" on pages 219–220 of *Lies Women Believe.* Do any of these apply to you? What are your personal "if onlys"—circumstances you blame for your wrong responses or your lack of joy?

_____

_____

3. What sinful responses have you been excusing or rationalizing because of circumstances beyond your control (e.g., I have not honored my husband, have spoken critically of him to others, and have been worrying because of his poor financial decisions)?

_____

_____

4. Give an example of a circumstance in your life that revealed something about your heart that needed to be changed (e.g., you become impatient while waiting in line at the supermarket).

_____

_____

5. Read 2 Corinthians 4:8–11, 16. How did the apostle Paul emerge from his circumstances as a victor, rather than a victim?

_____

_____

Respond

6. List one or more difficult circumstance you are facing at this time. Next to each circumstance describe your inward and outward response to that situation. God may or may not choose to change your circumstance, but if you will let Him, He will use your circumstance to change *you*. What changes are needed in your attitude or your responses?

_____

_____

_____

Day Two

Purpose in Suffering, pp. 221–3

Realize

1. List several different kinds of suffering that you or others you know have had to endure (e.g., financial disaster).

_____

_____

2. Give two or three illustrations of the natural human instinct to escape from suffering (e.g., divorce).

_____

_____

The Note from Nancy sidebar:

Note from Nancy

"All the New Testament authors recognized that there is a redemptive, sanctifying fruit that cannot be produced in our lives apart from suffering. In fact, Peter goes so far as to insist that suffering is our calling—not just for some select group of Christian leaders or martyrs but for every child of God" (p. 223).

3. Why is suffering an inescapable fact of the human condition? Will we ever be totally free from suffering and pain while we live in this world? Why not?

_____

_____

Reflect

4. What do the following verses in the book of 1 Peter teach us about the purposes of God in suffering and how we should respond to suffering?

- 1:7

_____

- 2:21–23

_____

- 3:9

_____

- 3:14–17

_____

- 4:1–2

_____

- 4:12–16, 19

_____

- 5:8–10

_____

5. Give an illustration of the "redemptive, sanctifying fruit" that suffering has produced in your life.

_____

_____

Respond

6. How could a painful situation you are facing at this time be for you "a pathway to sanctification and a doorway into greater intimacy with God" (*Lies Women Believe*, page 222)?

_____

_____

Lord, at times when I am hurting, my natural instinct is to cry out for relief.
But I don't want to forfeit the blessings that You can bring to me and to others
through my suffering. Thank You that You use suffering to make us more mature,
more like Your Son, who suffered for us. Help me to embrace the pain and
to allow You to fulfill all Your purposes in and through my life. Amen.

Day Three

Gaining an Eternal Perspective, pp. 223–6

Realize

1. Describe a time when you prayed for something, and it took God a long time to answer. (Or describe a prayer request you have been praying for a long time and are still awaiting God's answer.)

_____

_____

2. What do we learn from the following Bible characters?

- God promised to end Sarah's barrenness and give her and Abraham a child. How long did they wait for that promise to come true? (Genesis 12:4–5; 21:5)

_____

- How long was Joseph in prison (for a crime he didn't commit) after the cupbearer promised to bring Joseph's case to Pharaoh? (Genesis 40:23—41:1)

_____

- Joshua prayed for victory over his enemies. How quickly did God answer his request? (Joshua 10:12–14)

_____

- Mary and Martha knew that Jesus could heal their sick brother, Lazarus. How long did they wait before Jesus returned to them? (John 11:17)

_____

"*Your night of weeping may go on for months or even years. But if you are a child of God, it will not go on forever. God has determined the exact duration of your suffering, and it will not last one moment longer than He knows is necessary to achieve His holy, eternal purposes in and through your life*" (p. 225).

Reflect

3. What purposes might God have for not solving our problem or not changing our difficult circumstance as quickly as we wish? In what ways does God's waiting to answer our requests achieve His holy, eternal purposes in our lives?

_____

_____

4. According to Revelation 21:1–7, what do we have to look forward to? How can this vision help us to endure pain and suffering in this life here on earth?

_____

_____

Respond

5. Read Psalm 130:5. Waiting is a deliberate action that often requires more courage than taking matters into our own hands. It requires trust, obedience, hope, and perseverance. What is one current situation in your life where you need to simply and quietly wait on the Lord?

_____

_____

Father, sometimes it is so hard to endure when it seems like nothing is changing in my circumstances. Help me to wait for Your timing, Lord, knowing that You will act at the right time. Until then, teach me to trust, obey, hope, and persevere. Be glorified in my life, Lord. Amen.

Day Four

God's Grace Is Sufficient, pp. 226–8

Realize

1. Why do you think many people choose to just give up—on their marriages, their jobs, their children?

_____

_____

2. Describe a time when you were tempted to give up, throw in the towel, and say, "I just can't take any more." What caused you to feel that way? What did you do?

_____

_____

Reflect

3. Read 2 Corinthians 11:22–30. Do you think Paul ever felt like he just couldn't take any more? What do you think kept him going?

_____

_____

4. Now read 2 Corinthians 12:7–10. In what ways do you think Paul's "thorn in the flesh" was used by God? What did he learn about God's grace that he might not have learned any other way?

_____

_____

Respond

5. List two or three circumstances in your life that you cannot handle on your own. Then, write these words next to each circumstance: "Your grace is sufficient for me."

_____

_____

Lord, at times I feel that I simply can't take any more. I feel so very weak. Yet You promise that Your grace is sufficient for me and that Your strength is made perfect in my weakness. Help me to walk in Your grace and Your strength today. Thank You that, by Your grace, I can go on. Amen.

Day Five

Living a God-centered Life, pp. 228–35

Realize

1. Why are you alive? If you had to write a short life purpose statement, what would you say?

_____

_____

Note from Nancy

"Why was Paul able to sing hymns to God in the middle of the night in a Roman dungeon? . . . How could he 'rejoice always' when he was hungry and tired? His secret was that he had settled the issue of why he was living. He was not living to please himself or to get his needs fulfilled. . . . He had one burning passion: to live for the glory and the pleasure of God. All that mattered to him was knowing Christ and making Him known to others" (p. 230).

Reflect

2. According to Revelation 4:11, why were we created?

_____

_____

3. Read Philippians 1:21–24; 3:7–16. How would Paul answer the question, "Why are you alive?"

_____

_____

4. Read Acts 20:22–24. How did Paul's passion to fulfill God's purpose for his life enable him to endure and press on in spite of adversity?

_____

_____

Respond

5. What gets in the way of your being fully abandoned to Christ and His agenda in the world (e.g., particular people, goals, possessions, desires, etc.)?

_____

_____

6. Write a prayer confessing any areas of your life where you have been looking out for yourself and your own interests, and express your desire to live a life that is wholly centered on God.

_____

_____

_____

Lord, I confess that my natural tendency is to look out for myself, my interests, and my happiness. But I realize that it's not about me—it's all about You and Your kingdom, Your will, Your glory. I do not exist so You can make me happy. I was created to bring pleasure and glory to You and to reflect the light of Christ. I know that I will only find true joy as I lay down my life to that end. Amen.

1. In your reading and study of chapter 9, what truth did you find especially encouraging? (See pages 236–7 in *Lies Women Believe*.)

_____

_____

....

Lie: If my circumstances were different, I would be different.

Truth: My circumstances do not make me what I am; they merely reveal what I am. If I am not content with my present circumstances, I am not likely to be happy in any other set of circumstances. My circumstances do not have to control me.

....

2. The apostle Paul faced constant problems and adversity. However, his circumstances never diminished his joy. In fact, he had this extraordinary testimony: "I am exceedingly joyful in all our tribulation" (2 Corinthians 7:4 NKJV). How could Paul experience real joy in the midst of tribulation? (For some clues, see 2 Corinthians 1:3–6 and Philippians 4:11–13.)

_____

_____

Note from Nancy
"We have been deceived into believing we would be happier if we had a different set of circumstances. The Truth is, if we are not content within our present circumstances, we are not likely to be happy in any other set of circumstances" (p. 220).

3. When faced with stressful circumstances, Elizabeth Prentiss wrote to her friend, "The experience of the past winter would impress upon me the fact that place and position have next to nothing to do with happiness; that we can be wretched in a palace, radiant in a dungeon . . ." (*Lies Women Believe*, page 220). Why is this principle true? How have you seen this insight illustrated in your own experience or someone else's?

_____

_____

....

Lie: I shouldn't have to suffer.

Truth: It is impossible to be holy apart from suffering. True joy is not the absence of pain but the presence of the Lord Jesus in the midst of the pain. Suffering is a pathway to sanctification, a doorway into greater intimacy with God.

....

4. What blessings or benefits might we miss out on if we run from our suffering rather than embracing it and growing through it?

_____

_____

_____

5. Review the insights you recorded from 1 Peter on page 104. As you think about what you have learned about the purposes of God in suffering, how should that affect your perspective about a difficult situation you are currently facing?

_____

_____

Note from Nancy

"The Truth is, your pain—be it physical affliction, memories of abuse, a troubled marriage, or a heart broken by a wayward child—may go on for a long time. But it will not last forever. It may go on for all of your life down here on this earth. But even a lifetime is not forever" (p. 223).

Lie: My circumstances will never change—this will go on forever.

Truth: My suffering may last a long time, but it will not last forever. My painful circumstances will not last one moment longer than God knows is necessary to achieve His eternal purposes in and through my life.

6. Read James 1:2–4. What is the connection between trials and spiritual maturity? Why is it important for believers to learn perseverance, and how is it developed?

_____

_____

7. Read Romans 8:18 and 2 Corinthians 4:17–18. What hope do these verses give us? How does looking ahead help us face trials that seem to go on and on?

Lie: I just can't take any more.

Truth: Whatever my circumstance, whatever my situation, His grace is sufficient for me. God will never place more on me than He will give me grace to bear.

8. Ask two or three women in your group to share a brief example of how they found God's grace to be sufficient when they were facing a situation where they felt they just couldn't go on.

9. An important way we can minister to one another in the Body of Christ is to remind each other that the grace of God really is sufficient for all our needs and to encourage each other to exercise faith in His provision.

Provide an opportunity for any in your group who wish to do so to share in one sentence a circumstance that she is currently facing that seems unbearable at times (for example, "My son is addicted to drugs."). As each need is expressed, have the whole group respond aloud together, "His grace is sufficient for you." Then, have the woman who shared respond aloud to the group, "His grace is sufficient for me."

Then move on and let another share a situation for which she needs God's grace, and respond in the same way for each individual. (Don't whisper your responses—say with conviction, "His grace is sufficient!")

....

Lie: It's all about me.

Truth: God is the beginning and ending and center of all things. All things were created for His pleasure and glory. It's all about Him!

....

10. What difference would it make in our world if Christian women lived wholly for the glory and pleasure of God and the advancement of His kingdom?

_____

_____

11. How would your life look different if you lived this way?

_____

_____

Note from Nancy

"Whether I choose to believe it or not, if I am His child, the Truth is that 'His grace is sufficient for me.' . . . His grace is sufficient for every moment, every circumstance, every detail, every need, and every failure of my life" (p. 227).

CHAPTER

10

Walking in Freedom

In a Nutshell . . .

Chapters 10 and 11 conclude the book with advice about how to counter Satan's lies with God's Truth. The entire book is structured around these two related concepts: (1) Believing lies places us in bondage; and (2) the Truth has the power to set us free.

Some of us may need to address areas of deep-seated bondage. *All* of us need to be alert and on guard for Satan's lies. "Your enemy the devil prowls around like a roaring lion, looking for someone to devour" (1 Peter 5:8). His methods are cunning and deceptive. Knowing that most of us will not fall for outright lies, he feeds us subtle propaganda. Judging from the bondage that many women live in, he is doing a pretty good job of it. We see unhappiness, lies, and self-destruction all around us.

The good news is that the Truth is always stronger than any lie, just as our Savior Jesus Christ is always stronger than our Enemy. Believers are not immune to Satan's attacks, but we do have a weapon to protect us from them. We have the understanding of God's Word as absolute Truth. God's Truth alone has the power to help us discern Satan's lies and then set us free. Every time we hear a message directed at us, we should evaluate it in the penetrating light of God's Word. The more we study God's Word, the more the Truth will be in our hearts, on our minds, on our tongues. The better acquainted we are with His Word, the better we will be able to identify Satan's lies and bring to mind God's Truth.

When we learn the Truth, believe it, surrender to it, and live it, we will find ourselves set free. Then we can live the life Christ meant us to live—life abundant!

Exploring the Truth . . .

Day One

Surrendering to the Truth, pp. 243–52

Realize

1. Look through the forty lies listed in the table of contents for *Lies Women Believe*. During the course of this study, has the Lord shown you any specific areas where you have been deceived? List one or more lies (either from the list in *Lies Women Believe* or others that you have identified) that you realize now you have believed.

_____

_____

2. Illustrate how believing those lives has put you in bondage.

_____

_____

Note from Nancy

"The Truth has the power to overcome every lie. That is what the Enemy doesn't want you to realize. As long as you believe his lies, he can keep you in bondage. . . . The Truth has the power to set us free and to protect our minds and hearts from deceptive thoughts and feelings. . . . The Truth has the power to sanctify us—and to purify our minds, our hearts, and our spirits" (pp. 246–7).

Reflect

3. What corresponding truth from God's Word counters each lie you listed above? Write the truth(s) below, and note where you can find them in the Bible.

_____

_____

4. How can the truths you have identified set you free from bondage and sanctify you?

_____

_____

Respond

5. Just knowing the Truth is not enough. You must *surrender* to the Truth. What do you need to change in your thinking or your lifestyle that is not currently in line with the Truth of God's Word?

_____

_____

Lord, thank You for showing me the lies that have held me in bondage and
the Truth that can set me free. Please help me to surrender to and
act on the Truth every time a lie presents itself. Amen.

Day Two

Walking in the Truth About God, pp. 253–6

Truths 1–6

Realize

Rewrite each of the six truths listed on pages 253–6. Then look up the corresponding verses and describe how the verses confirm the truth.

Truth #1: Psalm 119:68; 136:1

_____

_____

Truth #2: Romans 8:32, 38–39

_____

_____

Truth #3: Ephesians 1:4–6

_____

_____

Truth #4: Psalm 23:1

_____

_____

Truth #5: Isaiah 28:16

_____

_____

Truth #6: Isaiah 46:10

_____

_____

Reflect

Complete this sentence: The truth that I most need to claim today is the truth that . . .

_____

_____

Respond

I surrender to that truth and will make the following changes in order to act upon the truth . . .

_____

_____

Lord, Thank You for Your Word that tells me the truth about who You are, what
You have done for me, and how much You love me. I claim the truth today that
_____ and surrender to that truth today by _____. Amen.

Day Three

Walking in the Truth of Christ's Sufficiency, pp. 256–9

Truths 7–11

Realize

Rewrite each of the five truths listed on pages 256–9. Then look up the corresponding verses and describe how the verses confirm the truth.

Truth #7: 2 Corinthians 12:9

_____

_____

Truth #8: 1 John 1:7

_____

_____

Truth #9: Romans 6:6–7

_____

_____

Truth #10: 1 Corinthians 6:9–11

_____

_____

Truth #11: Psalm 107:20; 119:105

_____

_____

Reflect

Complete this sentence: The truth that I most need to claim today is the truth that . . .

_____

_____

Respond

I surrender to that truth and will make the following changes in order to act upon the truth . . .

_____

_____

*Lord, Thank You that Your grace is sufficient to help me even in my deepest
need or strongest bondage. I claim the truth today that _____
and surrender to that truth today by _____ Amen.*

Day Four

Walking in the Truth by Relinquishing Control, pp. 259–62

Truths 12–17

Realize

Rewrite each of the six truths listed on pages 259–62. Then look up the corresponding verses and describe how the verses confirm the truth.

Truth #12: Philippians 2:13; 1 Thessalonians 5:24

_____

_____

Truth #13: Ezekiel 18:19–22

_____

_____

Truth #14: Galatians 6:7–8

_____

_____

Truth #15: Matthew 16:25; Luke 1:38

_____

_____

Truth #16: Ephesians 5:21

_____

_____

Truth #17: Titus 2:4–5

_____

_____

Reflect

Complete this sentence: The truth that I most need to claim today is the truth that . . .

_____

_____

Respond

I surrender to that truth and will make the following changes in order to act upon the truth . . .

_____

_____

Lord, Thank You that I can find joy and freedom by relinquishing control of my life to You. I understand that true freedom is found by submitting to You. I claim the truth today that _____ and surrender to that truth today by _____ . Amen.

Day Five

Walking in the Truth by Glorifying God, pp. 262–8

Truths 18–22

Realize

Rewrite each of the five truths listed on pages 262–8. Then look up the corresponding verses and describe how the verses confirm the truth.

Truth #18: Ephesians 5:25–27

_____

_____

Truth #19: Romans 8:29

_____

_____

Truth #20: 1 Peter 5:10

_____

_____

Truth #21: 2 Corinthians 4:17–18

_____

_____

Truth #22: Colossians 1:16–18; Revelation 4:11

_____

_____

Reflect

Complete this sentence: The truth that I most need to claim today is the truth that . . .

_____

_____

Respond

I surrender to that truth and will make the following changes in order to act upon the truth . . .

_____

_____

Lord, thank You that this life is a whole lot bigger than just me. I admit that often I am at the center of my own little world. The truth is, however, that I am not on this earth for You to make me happy; I am here to glorify You and bring You pleasure. That is what I want to do, Lord, today and every day of my life. As I do, You have promised that I will experience fullness of joy and the delights of Your pleasures. I claim the truth today that _____ and surrender to that truth today by _____. Amen.

Walking Together in the Truth . . .

1. What resources has God made available to protect us from deception? What are some practical ways we can guard our minds and hearts?

   _____

   _____

2. What have you learned in this study about Satan's lies and God's Truth that was new to you or that you needed to be reminded of?

   _____

   _____

3. How has your thinking changed as a result of this study?

   _____

   _____

4. Share a specific illustration of how the Truth has begun to change your life and set you free since you started this study.

   _____

   _____

5. It is not easy to walk in the Truth and to proclaim it to others. To do so requires that we swim upstream against the flow of our culture—and sometimes even against the flow of "Christian culture." List some biblical truths that fly in the face of our culture.

   _____

   _____

6. Why is it so important for believers to walk according to the Truth and to seek to point others to the Truth?

_____

_____

7. Share an illustration of how God used another individual to restore you when you were blind to the Truth or had wandered away from it.

_____

_____

8. Close your time together with prayer, thanking God for the riches and greatness of His Truth, freshly surrendering yourselves to live for His pleasure and glory and asking Him to use each of you to point others to the Truth that can set them free.

Note from Nancy

"In Christ and in His Word, we have the Truth that sets people free. That is Good News! And it is essential news. . . . We must learn the Truth, believe it, surrender to it, and live it out—even when it flies in the face of our culture. Then we must proclaim the Truth with boldness, conviction, and compassion, seeking to turn sinners from the error of their way and to restore those who have wandered from the Truth" (p. 252).

Dear Friend,

If this study has been meaningful to you, would you take a few moments to write me a letter and share how God has used it in your life? Here are some things you might want to include:

- Specific lies you realized that you have believed

- Consequences and areas of bondage you have experienced as a result of believing those lies

- Specific truths God has been using to set you free

- Any changes that have taken place in your life through the course of this study

- How God used this study in your small group

Once you have written your letter, you can either cut the page out of your book or make a copy and mail it to me at Revive Our Hearts, P.O. Box 31, Buchanan, MI 49107. Thanks for taking the time to share your story. It will be a great encouragement to me.

Gratefully,

Nancy

Nancy Leigh DeMoss

Dear Nancy,

Optional

Name *Miss/Mrs./Ms.* _____

Address _____

City _____ State _____ Zip _____

Phone (   ) _____ E-mail address _____

____ You have my permission to share my story with others . . .

    ____ with my first name.

    ____ without my name.

____ If you share this testimony, please change any details that could reveal my identity.

Suggestions for Group Leaders

Welcome to your role as a group leader. Perhaps this is a comfortable position for you—leading a group feels natural because you've done it for so long. Perhaps you are brand-new to this type of leadership role and feel unsure about how to begin. These suggestions are meant to remind you of some of the basics of leadership and to give you some specific ideas for leading the *Walking in the Truth* study. I pray that, as you take on this important role, God will give you wisdom and insight to help the women in your group comprehend and embrace the important truths you'll discuss.

This study serves as a companion to *Lies Women Believe*. The book addresses the whole concept of spiritual deception and exposes what I believe are some common lies that many Christian women believe. Some of the lies are obviously untrue but have been unconsciously accepted by many women. Other lies are more subtle or are half-truths, making them more difficult to identify. When we believe lies—whether overt or subtle—we ultimately end up in various types of bondage.

My desire is to see women identify the lies that have placed them in bondage and then counter those lies with the Truth that can set them free. *Walking in the Truth* is designed to help women go further in that process, through a ten-week study that includes personal study and application and, ideally, a weekly gathering in which women can share what they are learning with other women.

Discussing the Truth—Handling Differences

The first major purpose of the weekly group session is to provide an opportunity for women to discuss the material presented in each chapter and to develop a greater understanding of the Truth.

As you talk through the questions each week, remember that you are trying to help women get a broad overview of the major theme of each chapter. You are not trying to deal exhaustively with any of the specific topics. Some of the individual lies could take multiple sessions to cover thoroughly. Resist the temptation to give too much time to a single lie. Encourage the women to keep their answers brief so that you will not get stuck on any one question and so that as many women as possible can participate. (When introducing a time for discussion or testimonies, I sometimes tell women, "If you're having trouble landing your plane, I'm going to help you out!")

It is likely that there will be some disagreement on a few of the more controversial topics in the book. I understand that some sincere believers may not share some of my positions. Allow for honest discussion and disagreement. However, encourage the women in advance to do so in a spirit of humility and to avoid having an argumentative spirit.

Let the women know on the front end that you do not want to bog down on individual points where there may be differences. Explain to the women how important it is that they base their answers on the Word of God and not on their personal opinions or what they or others have always assumed to be true. Instead of saying, "I think . . ." or "I feel . . . ," encourage them to say, "The Scripture says here that . . ."

The ultimate goal of the study is not to get women to agree with you or me on every point but to get them to search out the Scripture for themselves, so they can learn to discern Satan's lies, to know God's Truth, and then to take the actions necessary to walk in the Truth.

Applying the Truth—Encouraging Participation

The second purpose of the group session is to provide an opportunity for women to open their hearts to each other, to share how they have been living out the Truth they have been learning, and to encourage each other to move forward in their walk with God. Clearly state from the beginning that any personal sharing is to be treated as private and should not be shared beyond the confines of the group.

Depending on the nature and extent of the lies that have been embraced and the bondage that has resulted, the book and this study guide may dredge up some deep-seated issues in some women; it may cause others to discover that they are not living the abundant life Jesus offers because they have believed a lie that they hadn't recognized; yet others may feel the need to reevaluate some of their unconscious beliefs. Every woman will respond differently.

Although you will want to encourage all the women to participate in the discussion and sharing, be sensitive to those who are not comfortable expressing themselves in front of others. If the women in your group do not know each other well or are unaccustomed to this kind of sharing on a personal level, they may be more reserved in the early weeks. Don't get discouraged. As they get more comfortable with each other, they will be more likely to open up.

At times, you may need to direct the conversation so that one "bleeding heart" doesn't dominate an entire hour. If you sense that someone is really struggling, you may want to offer to set up a time for the two of you to talk together. You may also sense that a more talkative person wants to spend extra time talking with you, too. It is important that your group meeting not turn into a therapy session. Ask the Lord to give you sensitivity and wisdom as you give direction to the discussion.

Allow the Holy Spirit to work with each woman individually. Some women may be quick to identify multiple issues that need to be addressed in their lives. Others may recognize that they have believed a lie, but it may take time for God to show them what changes they need to make (or for them to find the courage to make those changes). Others may require more time to identify the lies they have believed. Be patient with your group. Trust God to work in each life in His way and His time.

Preparation for Group Sessions

As a leader, you will need to do the study along with your group. As suggested in the Introduction, you need to read *Lies Women Believe* and complete the studies for each day between your group meetings. (It might be helpful for you to read the entire book ahead of time so you understand the big picture.)

Make sure that each member of your group has her own copy of *Lies Women Believe, Walking in the Truth,* and the Bible. Participants will need to complete the lessons for Days One through Five in each chapter prior to the group meeting. (They do not need to complete the "Walking Together in the Truth" section because you will cover those questions together during your group discussion.)

Encourage your group members to be consistent with their homework because they will get much more out of the study and the group discussions if they work through the lessons on their own. At the same time, you may want to acknowledge at your first meeting that some women may find it difficult to complete all the homework each week. Encourage them if possible to at least read the chapter before the group session, but let them know that they are welcome to attend, even if they haven't finished all the homework. It's more important that they hear the Truth than that they answer every question.

Structure and Format

Assuming there are several women in your group, an ideal time frame for the group session is two hours. Here is a suggested schedule if you have that much time available:

10 minutes	Fellowship (perhaps with light refreshments)
5 minutes	Welcome and opening prayer
5 minutes	Read "In a Nutshell"
90 minutes	Group discussion and interaction
10 minutes	Prayer time

If you are using this study in a Sunday school class or another setting where your time is more limited, you can adjust accordingly.

Regardless of your time frame, each time you meet, begin your time together with prayer. Then read aloud the "In a Nutshell" section, which is simply a brief overview of the chapter. This will help refresh everyone's memories as well as include those who may not have finished their homework.

The group discussion is intended to be an overview of the topic with a few questions devoted to each lie and the corresponding truth. Depending on how much time you have and how talkative your group is on a given day, feel free to pick and choose certain questions to discuss as a group. Some weeks you may cover all the questions, and other weeks your group may cover fewer questions.

Close your group time in prayer for one another. You can pray as a group or divide into pairs or smaller groups if that works better based on the number in your group.

Seeking Him for Change

As a leader, bathe each session and each of your group members in prayer. If possible, take time to pray each day for the women in your group by name. Ask God to open their eyes and hearts through the course of this study to whatever He might want to teach them. Don't make assumptions about the women in your group. The woman who appears the most put together on the outside may be covering severe struggles in her life. The quietest one may have the most depth. The loudest one may have the most needs. Ask God to give you discernment so that you can help meet their needs.

If a group member is struggling with a serious issue, you may want to privately recommend that she seek further help from her pastor or another spiritual leader in her church. Continue to offer God's Truth and encouragement, and pray that God will give you wisdom to lead the members of your group to His throne of grace, where they may obtain mercy and find grace to meet their need.

God promises that if we seek Him with all our hearts, we will find Him. His Truth is the greatest power for change in the universe. Expect to see lives changed through this study—including your own. God has the power to set us free to live an abundant life. I pray that you will experience His presence, His grace, and His Truth in a powerful way as you lead this group. May God richly bless your efforts!

Nancy Leigh DeMoss has produced numerous booklets, audiotapes, and videotapes to help women experience freedom, fullness, and fruitfulness through Christ. For a catalog of available resources, or to learn more about the ministry of Revive Our Hearts radio or conferences, contact:

Life Action Ministries
P.O. Box 31
Buchanan, MI 49107
(269) 684-5905
E-mail: Info@LifeAction.org
www.ReviveOurHearts.com